My Country, Canada or Quebec?

"Published on the occasion of the Centennial of Canadian Confederation and subsidized by the Centennial Commission".

"Ouvrage publié à l'occasion du Centenaire de la Confédération Canadienne, grâce à une subvention de la Commission du Centenaire".

Also by Solange Chaput Rolland
(in collaboration with Gwethalyn Graham)
Dear Enemies/Chers Ennemis (1964)

My Country, Canada or Quebec?

SOLANGE CHAPUT ROLLAND

> *The true spirit of democracy*
> *lies not only in recognizing*
> *equals but in creating them.*
>
> Gambetta

1966 Macmillan of Canada Toronto

Published simultaneously in the French language as
Mon Pays, le Québec ou le Canada?
by Le Cercle du Livre de France, Montreal

Printed in Canada

To Gwethalyn Graham
whose death obliges me
to write alone this diary
conceived for two voices.

Author's Note

Because this book is deeply concerned with biculturalism and bilingualism, I have decided to translate the French version of this diary myself, though I am fully aware of my difficulties with the English language. I beg the indulgence of my readers. I wish to thank Macmillan of Canada for having edited my English manuscript. I am particularly grateful to Professor W. L. Morton for writing the Foreword to the English edition and to M. Claude Ryan of *Le Devoir* for writing the Foreword to the French edition.

Solange Chaput Rolland

TORONTO
September 16, 1966

Contents

Foreword by W. L. MORTON

Solange Chaput Rolland needs little introduction to English Canadians. *Dear Enemies*, written with the late Gwethalyn Graham, has already made her known as an author of feeling and insight. She is a Canadian of French speech and culture who wishes to be accepted as such by English Canadians and as no less Canadian than they.

To introduce this diary of a journey to all parts of Canada may, however, serve a purpose. It may persuade English Canadians to read a frank, but not hostile, commentary on English Canada as experienced by a French Canadian.

I must first echo Mme Rolland's profound regret that the diary has not been written as planned, in company with Gwethalyn Graham. The untimely death of Gwethalyn Graham made that impossible. Yet I cannot help feeling that even in that sad loss there may have been some gain – gain that had better not have been, but still gain. Much of the dialogue that was planned, the softening and consideration that would have occurred between friendly enemies, has had to be foregone. And the rejection of English Canada with which this books ends, so deeply wounding to an English Canadian, might have been softened or averted. Yet something has been gained in singleness, in directness, and in cathartic rawness. In this diary Mme Rolland has woven, without trimming or softening, and in it she wears, the hair shirt all thoughtful Canadians today must wear.

This harsh and often irritating commentary is one for all tough-minded Canadians, and, by that sign, those who care for Canada must read it if they are to measure up to the condition of Canada today. It is a book that will shock, anger, and sadden. I introduce it and recommend it as such.

By doing so, I do not necessarily assent to any of its conclusions, or agree with its comments. Some of the former, and many of the latter, I would sharply disagree with and dispute with a vehemence perhaps to match the author's. That, however, is by the way. I respect Mme Rolland's honesty. I honour her strength of feeling. I am grateful for her penetrating insights, and above all her magnificent endeavour to hold all points of view, all sentiments of others, however prejudiced, in sane and balanced judgement. Here is a mirror, with surprisingly little distortion, held up to that fugitive and fearful thing, the English-Canadian mind. No man, I once remarked rather pompously to Mme Rolland, has encompassed this country. Could it be that a woman has? Certainly she has seen and felt and listened, and certainly she has spoken her mind.

Some questions an English Canadian must ask on reading this book. How terribly sad – and how very Canadian – that in the end the author concludes that what little hope there may be for her wishes and aspirations as a French Canadian lies in being a *Québécoise*. Quebec, she feels, may some day be a country, but Canada never. What, then, remains for English Canada? Nine wood-pulp republics increasingly Americanized? Or union by default with the United States? I lack Mme Rolland's courage but share her despair of English Canadians who are letting a splendid destiny perish for want of a little generosity of mind, a little grace of spirit, in dealing with Canadians as Canadian as themselves though different in speech and habit.

Must we not consider also, however deep our despair, that

neither English nor French Canada can in fact survive without the other? For French Canada, is not separation a counsel of despair which contradicts the French determination to take a full and free part in the modern world? Is it not also, for English Canada to deny French Canada a full and free role within Canada, to deny the very essence of Canadian national aspirations by invoking cultural continentalism, the fact that North America speaks English. This Professor D. G. Creighton has just done, and distorted by the act a lifetime of devotion to the understanding of Canada.

Again, is it not sad beyond words to realize from these pages that French and English Canadian co-exist but do not accept one another; that each has aggravated the other's defects and has not enhanced the other's virtues; that they have stultified, and not invigorated, one another?

And ought we not finally to consider that no political change, not even independence, can really make Quebec freer than it already is, and that if Quebec is resolved to be true to itself, so also is English Canada? And if each is to set itself to be true to itself, what can save Canada but frankness, candour, even brutality, of dialogue between those not afraid to speak out in English and French?

Such questions are raised by this courageous book. In writing it, Mme Rolland has, I believe, served the Centennial Commission well, and also Canada. May she always be happy in Quebec and one day, perhaps, at home anywhere in Canada!

*My Country,
Canada or Quebec?*

PREFACE

February 1966
LAC MAROIS
La Cédraie

The chips are down: I have accepted this morning the bursary offered in May 1965 by the Centennial Commission to Gwethalyn Graham and myself enabling us to continue the dialogue we began in *Dear Enemies*. We planned to tour Canada and write a diary, each expressing our views on this country as a French-speaking and English-speaking Canadian. The bursary was to pay the cost of a long journey carrying us from Newfoundland to the frontiers of Alaska.

Gwethalyn Graham died in November 1965. Her death leaves me alone, cut off from her friendship and her stimulating collaboration and I am forced to write alone a diary conceived for two. Because of this, my diary will become more personal, less objective. I am now faced with the question which has haunted me since the publication of *Dear Enemies*: Is my country Canada or Quebec?

A diary written alone or in collaboration is not necessarily a personal confession. But inasmuch as I have been influenced by certain personal experiences which have had a profound impact on my outlook, it might prove useful to relate the education I have received and to explain my own assessment of my country's destiny.

I am a French Canadian, passionately proud of belonging to the French community of this world. When I sing 'O Canada', I think of Quebec first because French was the first and only language of this country for more than two centuries, two centuries during which my ancestors mapped and explored. I think of Quebec first because this province is the only one in which I feel completely at home, the only one which allows me to live freely in French twenty-four hours a day.

I belong to a bourgeois milieu. My youth was without great joy but without pain. Adulated by parents strongly tied to the dictates of Church and social standards, I was brought up somewhat isolated from four older brothers who did not have much time to spend with a young girl already in revolt against this stifling milieu. I pursued my studies in Le Couvent d'Outremont, a private school, and at eighteen I went to Paris to study afresh what I had so badly learned in my province. During my stay in France, I foresaw my vocation as a writer, but it took seven years to fulfil my dream. My father, a man deeply rooted in culture and in politics, remained deaf to my wish. I dared not openly fight him; in my youth it was not yet in fashion to rebel against one's parents.

Married in 1941, I moved to St-Jérôme, a small industrial town. I am not particularly proud to confess my snobbery, my arrogance, my ignorance of the hard facts of life during my first married years. In order to fill my lonely hours in a St-Jérôme definitely hostile to my own hostility, I went back to reading. I underline the words 'went back', because my youth was uplifted by long and wonderful hours of reading. My father, who was a connoisseur of literature, had a curious way of saying, whenever he went out of the house: 'I have hidden the key to my book-shelf under the clock in the living room; I forbid you to read my books.' Thus, with his charming complicity, I had read most of his favourite authors at fifteen. I may not have grasped the meaning of these writers, but I have never lost my devotion to literature.

My work as a radio, TV, and newspaper journalist brought me in contact with the pluralist world and soon I discovered the frustrations of the underpaid – the hardship of the French-

3

Canadian working only in English in a Canadian industry. I also learned the history of Quebec and realized that most of our history books were not telling the truth about our good and supposedly saintly ancestors. At twenty I believed in Duplessis, as my parents did; at thirty, disgusted with patronage and compelled by an upsurge for freedom of speech, of thought, and of expression, I fought against him. In 1955, I founded *Points de Vue*, a political magazine, anti-Duplessis, pro-labour, deeply implicated in the creation of a system of neutral schools in Quebec, and strongly nationalistic besides. It was not particularly popular with our political and religious authorities.

I became a devoted nationalist following my experience as a journalist and as a lecturer in English Canada. Since the publication of *Dear Enemies*, I have pushed aside all my hopes of ever becoming a good novelist to 'plunge', as André Laurendeau once wrote, 'into the heart of our Canadian crisis'.

I do not relate my past for the dubious pleasure of exposing my private life to the public eye, but simply to point out that my opposition to English Canada does not rest on personal or family humiliations, but on a valuable knowledge of its books, its people, its way of life. My collaboration with the Toronto *Star* and my frequent trips in the English provinces have given me time to scrutinize the English-Canadian scene. Furthermore, I now live in Lac Marois, by a lovely lake reflecting peace and silence in our beautiful Laurentians; of the two hundred families gathered in this community, most of them from Montreal, three or four can manage a five-minute conversation in French with my son, my husband, and me. I am thus quite familiar with an English-Canadian environment, but whatever affection I feel for my English-Canadian friends, I am never completely at ease in their midst. One part of me is always absent from these meetings, because our ways of life touch only at certain points.

I am not a writer of any stature. I like to think of myself as a journalist passionately attached to 'la terre-Québec' and anguished by the foreboding of our difficult tomorrows. I do not find it enough to live *in* my country; I must live *with* my country to function on an intellectual and moral level. If I find English Canada ready to accept the French fact on this continent, I shall say it without fear of the sarcasm of some of my com-patriots, comfortably enjoying their revolution. If I discover no place for a stronger Quebec in a stronger Canada, then I shall also say that, calmly and without fearing to be called a fierce nationalist by those who have convinced me that I am a Quebec-ker first and last. I also realize quite humbly that whatever I write about my country will not change it. But all my life I have be-lieved that it is infinitely better to be mistaken in living up to my love for 'ma patrie' than to remain prudently right by never daring to commit myself.

A Dieu Vât.

NOVA SCOTIA
PRINCE EDWARD ISLAND
NEW BRUNSWICK

*If travellers were sincere
they would readily admit
their indifference to
sceneries. They are really
looking for human beings.*

François Mauriac,
*Nouveaux Mémoires
Intérieurs*

This trip begins oddly. I arrived at this airport at 6 p.m. to learn that flight 850 for Halifax will now depart at 11 p.m. I left my comfortable home on Lac Marois at three this afternoon and I will land in Halifax at three tomorrow morning.

I sit down at a table in the dining-room and as soon as I open the notebook in which I will record the events of this trip, I feel strangely at peace. Yes, Rainer Maria Rilke was right; I too would die if I could not write. I sort out my ideas, taking into consideration the wise advice of my editors. Suddenly I remember all that, at the same time, united and opposed them. Pierre Tisseyre of Le Cercle du Livre de France of Montreal, dynamic, easy to rouse, sure of himself, and Jim Bacque of Macmillan of Canada, calm, a little too serious for his age, and very much aware of the Canadian crisis. Both of them trust me and tonight, alone in the deserted airport, I suddenly feel oppressed by my responsibilities of writing this diary alone.

Suddenly my heart goes to Gwen. We had planned to leave together for the Maritimes. But if I permit her memory to burden my departure, the first pages of my diary will be overshadowed by a great sense of sorrow. I must turn the page.

'Why did you accept this difficult mission?' my friends asked. I do not know, and yet in some mysterious way I do. How could I live with myself if I did not once again try to bridge the gap between French and English Canada? My departure from Montreal gives rise to various comments from my French-Canadian friends, most of whom are separatists. 'So you still believe in English Canada's goodwill toward us?' – Yes I do, but less and less, I am afraid. My English-Canadian acquaintances view my trip with anxiety. Aware of my impatience with their comfortable position as a minority in Quebec, they fear my reaction as a French Canadian exposed to nine English provinces.

A woman sits at my table in the dining-room. We smile at each other, and open a conversation. My companion was born in Calgary, and does not speak French. Realizing my French identity a little too soon for my bilingual vanity, she naturally excuses herself for not knowing my language, thus projecting me instantly into the core of our problems.

'I learned French in High School. I can still read it, but I cannot speak it.'

How could she, since most of her teachers taught French without being able to speak one word of it? Every Canadian deplores the poor quality of French in English schools, but do we really try to improve the situation? I am aware of an awakening interest in bilingualism in most parts of English Canada, but I doubt if the desire to speak French is based on love for Quebec. Evidently my companion does not need French to live in Calgary. 'Russian, German and Ukrainian are more useful,' she comments.

Our dialogue slowly fades into silence. I am somewhat ashamed of my impatience with her explanations, but for years I have listened to many excuses about unilingualism and I am now unable to hide my annoyance when people apologize for their lack of French.

On the other hand, I admit that some of my English friends

have every right to be annoyed with my impatience when they laboriously try to speak French. But why have they waited until this country is about to explode to patronize Berlitz Schools?

At last, we are in the air. My stewardess, from England, soothes me kindly in 'frenglish', and offers me, as a token of Air Canada's respect for bilingualism, *Paris Match*! O Canada, land of our ancestors!

This trip would be so much easier if my name was Sue Rowland; I would not then fear being misunderstood, nor feel dispossessed of everything I hold dear. Less than twenty minutes from Dorval, I lose my name: I am now known as Soulange Chapoote-Rollande. I also lose my newspapers, my language, my Quebec magazines. Every traveller leaves his country behind when he travels abroad, but as a French Canadian, I become a stranger in my own land simply by crossing a street! All French Canadians feel this estrangement when they travel in Canada, and most of them resent it. I do too.

Out of compassion for my stewardess's kind efforts to speak French, I switch to English, already a little humiliated, a little angry because my plane still flies over Quebec, but fully conscious of the expediency of speaking 'the Queen's English'.

All towns look alike at three in the morning. I arrived alone in Halifax at dawn and I could have landed in Calgary, Edmonton, or Regina without realizing it.

I learn that the initiative for a French Week at Dalhousie University came from a law student from Jamaica. The English students were less interested, it seems.

A telephone informs me of the tragic death of Quebec's

Lieutenant-Governor. I have had the honour of being received at Bois de Coulonges and this news upsets me.

'The newspapers are talking about an explosion; do you think this fire may result from terrorism?' a reporter asks me. I answer that, knowing the Comtois family's popularity in Quebec, I cannot conceive any such crime against them. It seems too easy for most English Canadians to suspect Quebec of the worst motives at every incident. I end our conversation rather abruptly. And then a violent explosion throws me out of my chair, to the amusement of a friend.

'The gun of the Citadel fires at 12 o'clock.'

'Every day?' I asked, still trembling.

'Yes,' she laughs, 'for the last two hundred years.'

Here, at least, traditions are thundering!

Midnight
HALIFAX

Halifax is a peculiar town; the wooden houses all look alike. The people are somewhat grim, little inclined to be facetious. It must be difficult to be accepted here, but fortunately, through my long association with Voice of Women, old friends are helping me to meet the residents of Halifax.

A religious cleavage divides Halifax. Catholics and Protestants live in two ghettos and seldom meet. The Establishment, I am told, controls most of the social activities and some of the political thinking here. When I inquired timidly why the urbanists do not apply a little plastic surgery to the town, I am reminded that the Establishment owns here, as everywhere, the best lots and that they are not ready to sell.

A television show goes rather well. Why am I in Halifax? What kind of a book am I writing? Have I changed opinions on Canada since the publication of *Dear Enemies*? What does Quebec want? When will Quebec be contented? What are the solutions to our national crisis? Simple questions to answer in seven minutes! Finally I have to admit my ignorance concerning Quebec's attitude toward the Eskimoes, the Indians, and Labra-

11

dor's frontiers. I leave the studio rather deflated because I have not been able to explain clearly what Quebec wants along these lines.

Distressed, I realize my visit will implicate my friends.

'We will be considered pro-French,' they say.

'And is it a sin to be pro-French?'

'No, but it is compromising.'

With this blow to my pride, I inquire about this veiled animosity toward Quebec.

'Yours is a rich province, and ours is poor. Ottawa stoops down to you with all kinds of concessions; you have the power of blackmail and you use it well.'

Maybe I have discovered the core of the Maritimers' bitterness against us.

February 22
2 p.m.
CBC, HALIFAX

I am the guest of a young French-Canadian woman who teaches French to English children in Grade 7. Twice a week, on television, she reads, sings, and tells stories in French. I suddenly laugh because she says in mock despair: 'My staff of cameramen, producers, directors, and prop men have listened to these courses for over two years and they are still unable to speak one word of French.' I am beginning to wonder whether there is a congenital infirmity in most English-Canadian brains prohibiting them from being bilingual. While the crew is busy with cameras and lighting, I endeavour to analyse my reactions.

At nine this morning I gave a lecture to history students at Dalhousie. I had been warned by their professor of their possible resentment against Quebec, but I was delighted with their curiosity, their frankness, their honesty. I talked of Quebec and of our aspirations. Professor Rawlick drew a parallel between the Durham Report, which they are now studying, and the realities of Quebec's revolutions. I shouldered his views and tried to illustrate the demands of Quebec. During the question period I was forced to explain what I had just expressed five minutes ago. I am beginning to suspect my audiences throughout Canada of not listening to what I have to say. Usually someone says, 'Madame Rolland, you have just said that . . . .' I invariably have to answer, 'On the contrary I have just stated that . . . .' This same phenomenon applies to most newspapermen. They seldom report in their column what we say, but rather what they want to hear. The results are sometimes startling. For example, recently I answered a journalist that Quebec was not always eager to accept Rome's ruling in matters of religion. The next day to my amazement I read in the paper: 'Madame Rolland declares Quebec is against the Pope.' It was not very easy to come back to Quebec and to face irate curés after that incident!

I begged the permission of my class to ask the last question: 'What do you want or expect of Quebec?'

The answer was hard, blunt, and very honest.

'We want you to shut up and leave us alone.'

Needless to say, I was startled. The young student was, I realized, equally surprised at her own vehemence.

I left the class in good spirits in spite of this statement. Professor Rawlick was upset, but soon a current of friendship was established between us. I am not a detached and prudent lecturer: I speak bluntly and fully expect to be answered likewise. At the Faculty Club, I questioned another professor as to why the Halifax papers were so silent about the university's 'French Week'.

'Their attitude has nothing to do with a resentment against Quebec. Our newspapers seldom say anything anyway.' I am less sure their indifference applies to this case. Then he asked me to have breakfast with him the next day. 'There are a lot of things I would like to discuss with you, but please do not quote me.'

'Are you, too, afraid to be pro-French?'

'It would not be good for my job if I was suspected of leaning toward Quebec.'

It is painful for me to realize that an English Canadian openly on Quebec's side is ostracized in his own community. I remember Gwen's anger when some of her Toronto and Montreal friends accused her of not being a typical English Canadian because she was 'sold to the French'. I wonder if there is something contemptible in being known as a friend of Quebec.

The great mistake of this French Week at Dalhousie University, at which I am representing the Ministry of Cultural Affairs as a member of the Arts Council of Quebec, lies in the total absence of dialogue with the students. For many years I have often repeated that French and English Canadians should learn to speak *with* one another, rather than *at* one another. A lecture seldom permits a real conversation between the guest and his audience. But the students are eager to learn and they are soon on their feet, throwing questions to Professor Michel Brunet of the History Department of the University of Montreal. They seemed disturbed by the decision of our Quebec government to curtail the McGill grants. English Canada is up in arms because McGill University will now receive less money than in the past. Before my departure for the Maritimes, I had read in our newspapers the loud complaints of Ministers, professors, and students faced with the fact that Quebec was concentrating its grants on the French-Canadian universities. The secular poverty of Laval, Montreal, and Sherbrooke never bothered the conscience of English-Canadian élites, but when Quebec decides to help them first a great outcry of indignation befalls us. I am somewhat shocked by this cynical attitude – and I wonder what French Canadians living in the English provinces think of this reaction from Quebec's English minority.

10 p.m.
HALIFAX

A few hours ago, or was it yesterday, I described the angry reactions of the numerous students and ex-students of McGill at the announcement that Quebec had greatly reduced its grants to their alma mater. But even then I could not foretell that I would spend the rest of my day defending, in front of my audiences and on radio, not the decision of our government, for

I have no authority to do so, but the pressing needs of our universities. When I asked why it was normal for McGill to be wealthy while L'Université de Montréal was near bankruptcy a few years ago, I was answered: 'But it's not the same.' When I pressed for further explanations, I was then told: 'Since you people always complained about our injustices against you, take care not to commit any against us.'

After dinner, I talked with a group of twenty women interested in learning more about Quebec. After the inevitable inquiries about what Quebec wants, a woman suddenly said: 'I find you most unjust; the reason you speak English and neither we nor English Montrealers speak French is that you cannot earn your money in French while they or we don't have to speak your language to work in Canada.'

I tried as calmly as I could to say: 'You are right, madame, but this is precisely why Quebec is undergoing a quiet revolution. Since we are in a majority in Quebec, we ought to be able to earn our daily bread in French.'

'That has nothing to do with us here.'

Although I feel that it has, I am in Halifax not to reform the Maritimes but to explain Quebec's position and to hear opinions on Quebec. I went on to say that Quebec's revolution was directed not against English Canada but against the Establishment, French and English, in Montreal and in Quebec. I soon realized that my interlocutor could not understand why it was important for me to live a very French life in a very French province.

The end of this day finds me empty of feelings, of faith, of hopes. No, English Canada is not yet ready to yield one inch of its privileges to make room for us in Canada. The Canadian scene would indeed be more peaceful if Quebec could disappear from the Canadian map! I am not a separatist, not yet; but if I were to remain long in English Canada, I would become one in self-defence. I bear no racial prejudices in life. I abhor certain people not because of their racial or cultural types but simply because they hold certain arrogant attitudes which come into conflict with my own notions of democracy, of liberty, of courtesy. In Quebec, I flare up when some French Canadians condemn *a priori* all English Canadians. But as hard as I try to

15

remain objective and fair, here in English Canada I am bruised by the summary judgments with which many English Canadians reject us.

In Nova Scotia, I am particularly interested to note the open-mindedness of the Catholic clergy. The ecumenical spirit seems to be alive in this province.

But outside the clergy I have observed a timidity, a fear of being noticed, on the part of the Acadians.

'They have a broken spirit,' one of my companions commented. 'Did you know, for example, that less than twenty years ago, an average Acadian, meeting an English Canadian on the street, would instinctively tip his hat?' No I did not know, and I feel a twinge of remorse *vis-à-vis* my Acadian compatriots. And precisely at the very moment I write 'compatriots', I can well imagine their reactions! 'We are not French Canadians, madame, but Acadians.' They judge us severely for our carelessness with our own language.

'You jeer at our difficulty in speaking modern French, but last summer I sent my son to one of your camps in Quebec to improve his French. When he came back, he spoke worse French than when he left. Why?'

If our French in Quebec is not as pure as it should be, it is because for too long we were lazy, and we tolerated bad diction, poor pronunciation, second-class French. Today, Quebec is determined to purify its language, but we still have a long way to go before all our population will be able to speak an international French.

I am this morning painfully conscious that it will be impossible for me to pass an exhaustive judgment on Canada. Because of the limits of my Centennial grant, and because of my family obligations, I cannot reside very long in each province. Therefore I will accept humbly and readily the criticism of those who will surely ask how I can form an opinion of a town after spending so little time in it. But surely I can say that though there is a great difference between Vancouver and Halifax, this whole country becomes a monolithic block when it reflects on the situation of Quebec. I have been here for less than a week; already I have been told three times that 'Some of us are quite ready to go back on the Plains of Abraham and clean up your mess.' The young Jamaican student from Dalhousie who planned this French Week revealed that when he tried to obtain money from the big firms in Halifax, more than once he was asked, 'Why a French Week? The problem of Quebec was settled centuries ago, on the Plains of Abraham.' In short, a resentful audience in Alberta is the same as one in Halifax or Toronto. Almost everywhere in Canada, people asked me the same questions, and sadly I gave them the same answers. If only I could invent a country to permit me to renew my faith and my concept of democracy!

> *4 p.m.*
> HALIFAX

Last night at Dalhousie, Claude Ryan, editorial writer for *Le Devoir* in Montreal, addressed about five hundred students and told them in simple words what Quebec wants and does not want. This morning, the newspaper reported his magnificent lecture in a ten-line column, squeezed between reports of fires, false alarms, and temperature readings, on the last page. Many people complain about the lack of news about Quebec in their newspapers, but when the news is in their town, no one criticizes the bad reporting in the local press. There is a discrepancy between what people say and what they accept.

> *February 26*
> *8 p.m.*
> HALIFAX

Friday night, Pierre Laporte, Minister of Cultural Affairs for Quebec, was invited to address the last meeting of this French Week at Dalhousie, and he titled his lecture: 'Why a

17

special status for Quebec?' He was introduced to the students by Dalhousie's president: 'I am happy to greet the Hon. Mr. Laporte, but as president of this University I would like to state that I am completely against a special status for Quebec.' No one was surprised to hear the Hon. Mr. Laporte reply: 'I thank you, Mr. President, to allow me to state my case.'

A trivial incident, yes, but conclusive, *non*?

February 27
1.30 p.m.
AIRPORT, HALIFAX

I leave Halifax, very moved by the affection showered upon me by old and new friends, but at the same time a little bewildered because, though a resident of Halifax is a Maritimer first, he resents me for being, as a French Canadian, a Quebecker first!

February 28
CHARLOTTETOWN

Most Islanders reproach me because I have come to P.E.I. during the winter season. But fortunately or unfortunately, I am not here to rest or to enjoy the scenery.

Prince Edward Island's main sources of revenue are tourism and fisheries; both industries die out in the winter. Nevertheless, people here are friendly, eager to know visitors; their attitude toward Quebec is conditioned by the mass exodus of our population during the summer. How, in effect, do you despise a province that sends you more than 150,000 campers every year?

I am greeted at the airport by Jack MacAndrew, public relations officer at the Confederation Centre. For weeks I have succeeded in awakening in my heart a feeling of pride for this shrine. But I should have remembered with more humility my situation as the poor cousin of Canada! This huge cement citadel is a bit frightening. The art gallery will one day surely become one of the best in Canada, but it will be reserved for English-

18

speaking artists only. All posters, biographical notes on painters, sculptors, and artists, are in English. I visit the library and discover there is not a French book or a French newspaper or a French magazine. 'Every Canadian has invested about thirty cents of his budget in this national shrine through the grants of the provincial governments,' Jack MacAndrew tells me. Of course I sympathize with the lack of funds, and lack of planning for the Centre's future; but it would not take a crisis in Parliament to add a touch of French to this shrine – just a little courtesy, and about three hours of translation. The next day, I am called back to the Centre, and told that by some mysterious miracle money has been found to provide French posters for the summer programmes.

I am a little upset by this visit. Here at least, I would have loved to find some French other than Her Majesty's proclamation in the great hall. My country is decidedly Quebec. What choice do I have left?

11.30 p.m.

P.E.I.

I find it very hard, today, to smile freely. I walk around with clenched teeth, and with a bitter outlook because of yesterday's experience.

Fortunately this morning I breakfasted with Henry Wedge, Minister of Health in the Shaw Cabinet. This politician is open, free with his words, and does not seem to mind being quoted in my diary. We discuss the plight of Quebec and he tells me that if he were in our premier's shoes he would act exactly the same with Ottawa.

At ten, the premier, Walter Shaw, receives me with cordiality, friendliness, simplicity.

'And why are you visiting P.E.I.?'

'To find out, Mr. Premier, if your island is ready to make room for us in Confederation.'

I am literally deluged in a flow of words from the premier. He affirms his admiration for Jean Lesage and stresses the fact that his province would be happy to obtain the 'same concessions

19

from Ottawa that your people always get'. I wince at the word 'concession', and noticing my tenseness, the premier assures me of his admiration of 'your people, and your culture, which should be preserved in Canada. But', says the premier, 'you should tell your people that bilingualism works both ways.' I am speechless. It seems that Mr. Shaw could not find at the border of Quebec and New Brunswick a single waitress to speak English to him. 'If you want us to speak French, then you should learn English.' I tried to explain, in English, that we did not want to force French on English provinces, but to no avail.

On the island, religious segregation definitely exists as everywhere else in Canada. For centuries, we have pretended to respect our neighbour's beliefs. We all know that religious conflicts exist in Canada, and that more than problems of language they have set Canadians one against another. But of course we prefer to remain silent on this ugly form of discrimination. The ecumenical spirit has bridged some of this gap between religions, but our religious fights have left deep scars on the conscience of our nation. When, for example, one learns that in Ottawa a Catholic Minister, French or English, cannot appoint a Catholic under-secretary, French or English, one wonders why.

Religious struggles may not always take on national significance, although they hurt simple and worth-while citizens. Last night I went to a fishermen's village located eighty miles from Charlottetown. I visited with the Mother Superior of a convent and had a long conversation with her.

'Here, to succeed, we must be forgotten, we must not be conspicuous with our demands, nor with our rights. One night there was a dance in the Civic Hall. At the end of the evening, a violent storm arose, and the taxi driver did not want to take the chance of driving the young girls back home. Our convent was convenient, because it was so near. But when the girls learned they were to come here for the night, they simply refused to sleep at the Catholic convent. They were afraid of us,' she said sadly.

'Were you very hurt, Mother?'

'Yes, but we cannot blame our young people for repeating and feeling what they have heard for years.'

Et voilà! A little incident, in a little village, in a little island. No one will ever comment on it, it is of no national importance, but in how many places in Canada would I discover this resentment toward nuns and priests who are doing their best to give a good education to their pupils under impossible circumstances?

I came back in silence to my hotel. Though my English friends who had accompanied me could not understand a word of my French conversation with the Mother Superior, they sensed my emotions and respected them.

There is great excitement about the causeway to be built between New Brunswick and Prince Edward Island, but though the Islanders fully realize the progress this link with the mainland will bring them, they are at the same time afraid to lose the security of their insular existence. If this causeway is ever built, I hope the beauty of this Island will be protected, and I pray that hot-dog and French-fried-potato stands will not mushroom along the beaches as they have done on our beautiful Gaspé coast.

March 2
HALIFAX-FREDERICTON

We are grounded for an hour in Moncton airport. I have the bewildering sensation of waiting for I do not know what! In less than an hour, I shall meet new faces, ask more questions, and probably repeat the same arguments. . . .

March 3
FREDERICTON

Fredericton is prey to a curious hysteria, it seems. The Robichaud plan for social reforms is strongly contended by the Irving Trust and the Establishment. 'They will not win, madame, they must not win,' repeated some students who came to talk with me in the hotel. From them I learned a great deal of the political situation of New Brunswick and once again I marvel at the seriousness of our young generation who are able to look

21

into the future of this country with a deep sense of involvement.

A lovely young Acadian girl accuses me of being unconscious of her people's plight, of bearing contempt for her language. Once again I stumble against the deep and sometimes unconscious resentment of the Acadians for Quebec. I am ill at ease because we French-speaking Canadians set a poor example to our young students of the *bonne-entente* between French people in Canada.

'You speak loudly in Quebec and sometimes unwisely. And your young people do not care much for us, nor for the consequences of their attacks. The more they yell, the more we are persecuted here.' The bitterness of her words startle me.

'And what do you wish of Quebec, mademoiselle?'

'Nothing, except a little more maturity in your demands to the rest of this country.'

Some of her reproaches are well earned; too often, our compatriots living in minority groups throughout Canada are made to bear the brunt of Quebec's errors. When, for example, separatists demonstrate, when terrorists throw bombs, when young students riot with bad manners during the Queen's visit, French Canadians outside Quebec have to pay the price.

'The Acadian became prudent through forces of circumstance; he has felt inferior since the expulsion, and it has always been *l'autre* who takes the initiative. Silence is the secret of our survival,' a schoolteacher says bitterly.

'We are pragmatists, madame,' claims a young politician. 'We do not demonstrate at every occasion, but instead we act sensibly, moderately, prudently, and thus we obtain justice.'

It is not for me to point out to him that his appraisal of justice for the Acadians does not exactly seem right.

'Of course,' he continued, 'we have yet a long way to go.'

'Are your young people happy?'

'Our young people are at last growing impatient with their elders' prudence. But if the Acadians support Robichaud's platform openly and enthusiastically they might well harm him politically. Our drama consists in the absence of real Acadian leaders.'

'This is the drama of Canada,' I observed.

I meet some journalists and they all seem cautious; they are more or less stifled by the Irving interest which controls most of the mass communications here. The only semi-independent newspaper, the *Gleaner*, sold thirty-five per cent of its shares to Mr. Irving.

All this brings me to ask an intellectual if he believes in a fusion between Nova Scotia and New Brunswick, as has been rumoured since 1865.

'Such an alliance would not help our finances,' he says.

'Maybe not, but it would surely stop New Brunswick from becoming a second French province in Canada.'

'Your observation is very interesting,' he concluded.

10 a.m.
FREDERICTON

'Please bring New Brunswick's French newspaper,' I told the maid.

'What is the name of it?'

'How long have you been living here?'

'All my life,' she answers with the conviction of her forty-odd years.

'The name is *L'Evangéline*.'

March 5
FREDERICTON-MONTREAL

I have discovered a strong tie with the past in the Maritimes, in spite of their efforts to harness industry and commerce to modern times. The link with Great Britain is still strong among the loyalists and the Orangists, more active here than in the rest of Canada. How strange to realize that at both ends of our country, two provinces have developed strong affinities with the United States. Nova Scotia and British Columbia are pro-British and pro-American. The wealthy people, I was told, send their sons from Halifax to Boston, from Vancouver to Seattle. And both these provinces bear a resentment toward Quebec.

I had a pleasant lunch with Jack MacAndrew, who came from Prince Edward Island to seek advice on a French Week in the Confederation Centre. I had expressed, during my trip to Prince Edward Island, my disappointment in the unilingual aspect of our national shrine. Therefore I should not remain silent about their evidence of goodwill in improving this situation. Their posters for the summer Theatre Festival have been not simply translated, but recreated in French. Thus it sometimes pays not to let oneself be intimidated by men and events!

ONTARIO

*True generosity does not
satisfy itself in accepting,
but in giving.*

Georges Bernanos

Bilingualism aboard this train is pleasant, if mathematical. Suddenly I laugh because I notice, on the wall in front of me, a beautiful print of Montreal by my young friend Richard Lacroix, and on the opposite wall one of Toronto by an artist whose signature I cannot read. Mr. Gordon has learned a lot since the day Montreal students burned him in effigy because he said in Parliament that no French Canadians were qualified for higher jobs in his railway. The CNR has since been very respectful of its French 'voyageurs', and I am grateful for such courtesy.

I sometimes fume when English Canadians refer to Quebec as a priest-ridden province, but I am as impatient with French Canadians when they predict: 'You will stay one week in

26

Toronto, but you will die of boredom.' I will not. I know of several towns in Quebec in which I would not reside three hours! Toronto is one of the most beautiful cities in Canada. For ten years, she has undergone a great deal of reconstruction, and the results are impressive. Food is now quite good, but the prices are extravagant. Museums, art galleries, theatres, concert-halls are patronized by all the Torontonians. French Canadians must bring their appraisal of this city up to date. Toronto is no more saintly, pure, or puritan than Montreal is subservient to the call of its hundreds of church-bells! Yes, Sunday in Toronto is still an ordeal, but if one is alert, it is always possible to order wine, beer, or whisky the night before, and to spend a quiet Sunday afternoon visiting the Royal Ontario Museum and discovering one of the most valuable collections of Chinese art in the world.

The Torontonian is rather prone to view himself as the typical English Canadian. The CBC in Toronto expresses itself as if its broadcasts were speaking for the whole of the country, and this infuriates the other provinces. When I queried an old friend as to the common denominator of English Canadians coast-to-coast, she answered seriously: 'Their hatred for Toronto.' To be honest, I must admit that Torontonians are not very tolerant of other Canadians, and especially of English Quebeckers. They judge them harshly. And suddenly I remember the words of Lieutenant-Colonel Yves Bourassa, a publicity adviser for many agencies in Canada: 'You can say what you want in Toronto; the Torontonian will always listen to you quietly, politely, attentively, because he is absolutely convinced that you are not speaking of him but of somebody else.'

I do not expect Toronto to become suddenly pro-French, but at least I hope to find here a reasonable awareness of Quebec's life, thoughts, and aims.

March 28
6 p.m.
TORONTO

Two hours of intense, fluent, and frank discussion on the inevitable amendments to an already obsolete constitution

27

'submitted to great pressures from the American way of life'. I listen carefully to my political friend; I know how deeply involved he is in the future of this country and I am moved by his sincerity. 'Our English system of parliamentary rules, imported from England, does not answer the needs of this country, whose ideals are influenced by the U.S. In the near future, we will have to adopt the American federalism. Our governments will fall under partisan pressures and its decisions will be encumbered by traditional rulings. We should meet modern times with modern structures of democracy.'

'Your compatriots will never agree to sever their umbilical knots with England.'

'They will have to, if they want to survive as an independent nation. A republican Canada is the only answer to a republican America. Sometimes it is wiser to fight the adversary with his own weapons.'

'But English Canadians nearly suffered a collective heart-attack because Parliament adopted a distinctive flag for Canada. They will never reject the British Parliamentary rules. Once again we would have to live through months of national hysteria. And a country that gives itself the luxury of crying over its natural evolution is not yet a country. It is a colony desperately hanging on to its fear of independence,' I reply.

During the famous flag debate I read Hansard, and since those days of pathetic outcry I seldom talk of Canadian political maturity. But the words of my companion set me thinking. They help me to understand why so many French Canadians transplanted to Ottawa seem prone to commit errors, to become pale shadows of themselves. They are more or less crushed by the federal system.

'And do not forget', adds my friend, 'that this system was devised for a unilingual, small, and monarchical country.'

I am not qualified to express a valid opinion in such a field. I have not yet had the occasion to study the American system of federalism; but as a French Canadian, I would fear its tradition of assimilation. If we leave Charybdis for Scylla, we will just translate into an American vocabulary all the difficulties of bilingualism and biculturalism. Would our government

28

be more stable if we were to elect a president rather than a prime minister? Would Canada vote spontaneously for a French Canadian as prime minister if he were the better choice for our nation?

'What role will Quebec play in your republic?' I ask.

'Quebec is facing a difficult choice. Either you will pay the price for independence and accept fully the consequences of the economic recession that will undoubtedly follow, or you will adopt a new constitution leading the country to the American system of federalism. There is no other choice,' he concludes. 'English Canada, as it is, will make no more concessions.'

Nor will Quebec.

March 30
Noon
TORONTO

A long discussion with the managing director of the French radio station CJBC reveals the wonderful change of climate in Toronto. Two years ago, I had been a witness of the collective hysteria of Torontonians discovering that the CBC had decided to transform CJBC into a French-language station.

'It was as if we had become an oriental menace. The Orangists of Toronto were outraged because they thought we in CJBC were undercover papist agents,' laughed one young French reporter.

The Torontonians who generally ignored CJBC became fervent listeners when it was decided to have the station join the French network. But this morning Marcel Bourbonnais, manager of CJBC, let me read some letters from English listeners who confessed that they had been opposed to this station's becoming French but were today 'happy with this change'.

'CJBC is now popular in Toronto?'

'Yes. It is now quite chic to listen to our programs.'

'Is CJBC well supported by the Franco-Ontarians?'

'Yes.'

I ask this question because Torontonians have often com-

29

plained about the lack of dynamism of their Franco-Ontarian minority: 'Where are those French Canadians?' I have been asked many times. 'We never see them, never hear of them.' The Franco-Ontarians do not live in a ghetto atmosphere. They are widely dispersed in Ontario, as in Toronto. They do not know each other and for this reason seldom meet. But since the creation of a French station, they have found a voice, a rallying-point.

'We broadcast their meetings, their activities, we interview their leaders. We are their platform and they are happy with us,' pointed out Mr. Bourbonnais.

I am very happy to hear this. I am fully aware how painful it is for my French compatriots in Ontario to be criticized by Quebeckers whose existence has always been easy compared to theirs. But I feel the urge to say: 'If you want not only to survive, but to live your French destiny fully, then stand up, and speak loudly, calmly, but with a strong and united voice. Fight for your rights, but not only as if they were a privilege. Widen your culture, purify your French. In twenty years from now, there will be no place in Canada or in the world for small islands of francophones: our French language will not be Parisian but must become international.'

The French minorities have to choose between assimilation, which will end all their troubles, or the complete re-evaluation of their culture, their mother tongue, their attitudes. It is possible, yes, to be French *and* Catholic, but the two do not necessarily go together. The French-Canadian diaspora must break its ties with its priests in the areas of education, politics, and constitutional rights. For too many years they have been led by the Church though some priests could not always be right in matters remote from their religious knowledge. The day has come for French Canadians to bring out into the open their justified anger.

Who would believe this in Quebec, or in France for that matter! I am sitting in Toronto's Café de la Paix, and in order to escape from my English environment I slowly sip a café Cappucino. Wonderful sensation of being I don't know exactly where.

I read the *Star* and the editorial comments on Quebec Liberals' federal motion concerning the adoption of French as the second official language of Ontario and New Brunswick. From where I stand, this resolution appears immature and will serve no good purpose. French Canadians never miss an occasion to accuse Ottawa of infringing on purely constitutional provincial autonomy; they are now guilty of committing exactly the same sin in Ontario. This motion is, I suspect, designed more to win favours from the separatists than to really serve the cause of national unity. It will only harden against bilingualism those who already have not accepted French as a language of Canada. If the Quebec federal Liberals had invited some important Anglo-Canadian personalities to their convention, and if all of them had recommended French as the second official language of Ontario and New Brunswick, they might have made sense. As it is, this motion appears childish, ridiculous, and absolutely futile.

This afternoon, Bob Fulford, journalist, Ramsay Cook, professor of history at the University of Toronto, and Jim Bacque from Macmillan, gathered in my suite to discuss Quebec and its place in Confederation. We four have known each other for years, and our discussion, though blunt and honest, always remains friendly.

Ramsay Cook feels that Quebec does not quite know where

it is going. His book *Canada and the French-Canadian Question* is one of the best ever written on our national dichotomy. I do not agree with all his views concerning the British North America Act, for I believe that since the actual constitution has permitted certain abuses to be perpetrated against French Canadians, nothing will now stop English Canadians from passing new amendments to stifle Quebec's revolution.

But still, I would have loved to have been a student of Ramsay's. In my youth, history was not a favourite subject of mine and the way it was taught did not inspire me to extend my knowledge of my past. With Ramsay I dare not hold a long discussion, for his knowledge of history shames me.

Bob Fulford speaks with enthusiasm of his trade as book reviewer. To analyse a book a day for the *Star* seems quite a feat to me. I ask him if he could read a Canadian-written book without knowing who the author was and guess whether it was by a Westerner or an Easterner. 'The story might be the same, but the style of writing would not be,' he says. I am doubtful of the first part of this statement. Had Hugh MacLennan lived in Vancouver, would he have written *Two Solitudes*?

I then review the situation in Quebec, and thinking of the numerous books published by Peter Desbarats, Hugh Mayers, Thomas Sloane, Mason Wade, Frank Underhill, W. L. Morton, etc., I ask why so many English Canadians never read them.

'Our books are too dull,' one of them says.

'Your editors are afraid of bold books,' I venture.

Jim Bacque roars with indignation, and without answering his protest I take much pleasure in recalling that the two bestsellers of the year, *In Praise of Older Women* and *The Trial of Steven Truscott*, were both originally turned down by Canadian publishers. Isabel LeBourdais went to England to find a firm unafraid of libel suits, and Stephen Vizinczey underwrote his own novel. If a nation has the literature it deserves, it also has the publishers it merits. Our publishers in Quebec are surely not more mature, more intelligent, more alert than those of English Canada, but they are more implicated in their milieu. In general, English-Canadian publishers are less likely to take chances, to sponsor a new author, than French-Canadian firms.

They are cautious, conservative, and very conscious of 'respectability'. Jacques Hébert established a precedent by publishing at a low price *Les Insolences du Frère Untel*, which sold more than 150,000 copies. Other Quebec editors have followed his lead. They have printed bold books, many of them political essays, and our public, shocked by the angry young Quebec authors, have responded quite well. It is not rare for a novel or an *essai* to sell more than five thousand copies a few months after publication. Whereas years ago a Quebecker was elated when he was able to publish his work in France, today he chooses a Quebec publisher.

Our discussion turns to religious conflicts in Canada. Ramsay Cook thinks they are important 'but they do not form the core of our problems'.

Once again, I humbly disagree. Everywhere I have been in recent years, I have come across such conflicts. Of course, they are not always brought out in the open. In this country people usually are prudent in their dealings with the Establishment of the church, and those who dare probe this question often find themselves ostracized by their own compatriots.

I am well aware of an ecumenical spirit among the churches in Canada, but as in politics, I suspect that this openness and tolerance are found at the summit only. I wonder if between an average Catholic and an average Protestant there exists a feeling of kinship. How many times have I heard friends of mine remark good-humouredly, 'I would not mind my daughter marrying your son, for example, but I would wish he was not a Catholic.' And strange as it may seem, I am beginning to feel that in Quebec there is now more religious tolerance than in other parts of Canada. The quiet revolution stems in part from our revolt against our church, and because we are fully aware of our past religious despotism, we are becoming more open-minded.

The four of us are familiar with the press, and we proceed to look into the mass media of information and wonder if our newspapers, our radio, and our TV network are really doing a good job of informing Canadians about each other. We deplore the quest for sensational news, for blowing incident into main crisis, for twisting the words and attitudes of politicians French

33

and English. But I am a little tired of hearing the press blamed for all the troubles in Canada. Our colleagues are the product of our milieu: they are supposed to throw light on Canada, but they also are influenced, moulded, by our society and its imperatives.

Yet, here in Toronto can we refuse to applaud the *Star* and the *Globe and Mail* for their honest effort to explain, understand, and analyse Quebec's aims? The quality of their editorials has done much to bridge the gap between Quebec and Ontario. It is now possible to predict that if our Canadian dichotomy is to find a happy solution, it may be because Ontario leads English Canada into an acceptance of Quebec's position in Canada. I do not for one minute forget, however, the entrenched hostility to Quebec still existing in some parts of Toronto. Yes, the *Star* and the *Globe* are doing their best to buttress some of our views, but since my arrival here I have read numerous letters from irate readers all wishing that Quebec would get out of Confederation.

A French Canadian like me, who is looking for fraternity and love, sometimes breaks her heart on the contradiction of our leaders. Last night for example, the *Telegram* reported the words with which Lester Pearson ratified his government's desire to establish bilingualism as a fact in the Civil Service. In the next column, the *Telegram* informed us that in some parts of Winnipeg, schools were told to ease up on French, and the journalist went on to observe that these were the schools attended by French-Canadian children. So, once again one feels obliged to ask, Who is sincere in English Canada? At one end of the country, the central government officially recognizes French as a compulsory language in the Civil Service, and at the other end, another government does its utmost to reduce French in the French-Canadian schools.

Toronto is flowering this morning with hundreds of yellow daffodils. One flower is sufficient to put sun and light in my day.

I like to meet a journalist who is pretty, very feminine, unafraid to speak her mind and to fight for her ideas. June Callwood, journalist, writer, and panelist on television, is an exception to my view of the average Canadian woman. If in the past French and English Canada were admirably represented by courageous and intelligent heroines, now too many of them seem more interested in kitchens and social work than in expressing their views on Canada. I am deeply shocked to find so few of them on the front line of politics: are the women of Canada so little concerned with the future of this country that they refuse to help shape a harmonious world for their children and grandchildren? Of course I am aware of many in the arts, in social welfare, in theatre, but too few are willing to accept responsibility on the national scene. For one Gertrude Laing, sitting with charm and authority on the Royal Commission on Bilingualism and Biculturalism, how many great hostesses or rich women dare one original thought on Canada? June Callwood is one of those rare career women who are busy twenty-four hours a day but are always able to find a twenty-fifth to espouse a good cause. I am more than grateful that she 'invented' time for me.

We chattered without reserve, both aware that honesty is the only way to friendship.

'Why is there such a difference between our own deductions from income tax for charitable purposes and yours?' June asks. 'This discrepancy is difficult to understand in Ontario.'

It is difficult to understand in Quebec too. Unfortunately our education has always been concerned with religious rather than secular morality. By nature, and through a strange form of rebellion against the authorities, the average French Canadian thinks nothing of deceiving the State and the Church in matters of income-tax receipts. Though my explanation is lame, it is the

35

only one I can offer. But I could of course point out many rich English Canadians who have also cheated on their income tax and not always for charitable purposes.

'Why,' asks June, with her customary frankness, 'is your political code of ethics so different from ours?'

Once again, I must answer her honestly. I could, here again, point out that in many provinces political scandals have darkened the atmosphere, but what would I gain for Quebec by listing the names of politicians implicated in shady transactions throughout Canada? French Canadians are no more inclined to political immorality than their English counterparts, but they are less discreet about it. Many French Canadians deplore the ease with which some of our own politicians blunder into wild statements, or stoop down to trivial speculations. I make no excuses for them, but I recall once again that the difficulties of some French Canadians started at the Conquest. This is not a whining refrain, but a psychological truth. The French Canadian has been a colonial all his life. Before 1763, he was in servitude to the French lords; after the Conquest, he became the serf of his English masters; and for more than a hundred years, he was bishop-controlled. It would have been a miracle if such an alienation of his liberties had not had a profound impact on his social behaviour. As a result, the French Canadian came out strongly for collective rather than individual rights. Stifled by such pressures, he turned to politics for revenge and for recovering some of his lost prestige. Thus his own government was turned into an object of revenge, not only for his people *vis-à-vis* the English, but to give him power. This is not a cheap trait of character inherent in the French Canadians: it is a normal process of evolution in a conquered nation. Because so many French Canadians were one day dispossessed and ruined, they thought nothing of depriving others. It explains why today it is so easy, in the moral sense, to sell one's vote for a frigidaire or an absolution. The Church, certain of dominating its flock, closed its pious eyes on such abuses. Few French Canadians can recall without shuddering the terrible remark of Duplessis: 'I have the Bishops in the palm of my hands.' It was true for too many years.

36

Paul Fox, professor of political science at the University of Toronto, asks me to report the case of one woman in Scarborough who asked him for the name of a summer camp in Quebec. She wanted her son to stay in Quebec and learn more of our way of life. Professor Fox is happy with this request; he sees in it a hope for a bilingual tomorrow.

I am touched by this woman's effort, but I cannot honestly write pages and pages on this subject. For years, French Canadians who could afford it have been sending their sons and daughters to Ontario or British Columbia to master English.

'You are unfair,' Paul Fox will say. Yes, I am. But why should I marvel because some English Canadians are at last becoming realistic. To learn French is not a major accomplishment or a heroic act; it is a civilized way to live in an uncivilized country.

This morning I visited the French School of Toronto. I am full of admiration for the ease with which all these very young Torontonians are learning French, but I would have been elated if I had found that this French School, inspired by France, had adopted a few Quebec books as part of its curriculum. This kind of international bilingualism has no Canadian reality.

True, I realize that these fortunate children, most of them coming from Toronto's best families, do not need to know Quebec's history to succeed in life – but if one of them should aspire to become Prime Minister of Canada, it would be useful for him to know that in 1966 Quebec was still in Confederation.

'Quebec's school-books are too religious,' I was told.

This was true a while ago, but 'saintly Quebec' has changed too.

'Yes,' says Mr. J. C. Lockwood, president of Lever Brothers, 'we businessmen are fully conscious that Quebec is not a province like the others. Our products take into consideration the special needs of Quebec.'

I learn, for example, that Lux soap does not smell the same in Quebec as it does in the rest of the country. I try hard to philosophize on this subtle distinction, but I can't quite succeed.

We discuss the businessmen's role in Canada. I ask him if he is conscious of an obligation to participate in our national life.

'Political implications are always dangerous to our market.'

'But if Quebec were to secede, your market would suffer more.'

Too many industrial magnates are content to sit on the boards of many companies, but are reluctant to speak up for Canada and its political crisis. Nevertheless I am going to quote Mr. Lockwood's words; they should be repeated over and over again among English-Canadian leaders. 'Let us not forget that when Mr. Bennett or Mr. Roblin or Mr. Robarts takes a tough line with the federal government, we admire him for defending local interest. But when Mr. Lesage does so we accuse him of shaking the very foundation of Confederation.'

April 3
1 p.m.
TORONTO

I am perpetually astonished by Pierre Berton's vitality. He is the dynamic expression of one of my favourite theories: the more one is occupied, the more time one has for other people. In spite of his numerous TV, radio, and writing assignments, Pierre Berton receives me with friendship. He seems as relaxed as if he had nothing else to do than to talk about Canada and Quebec with me.

Suddenly he declares: 'The best way for Canada to fight the American influence would be for all of us to speak French only.'

He then discusses the astonishing about-turn of the Toronto

Star and *Globe and Mail* on the subject of Quebec. I confess my surprise at having discovered a bewildering combination of attitudes in Toronto. Here, it is not unheard of to be anti-war in Viet Nam, for civil rights in the U.S.A., and for Quebec in Canada.

'You are now in good company,' observes Berton. 'This is a healthy sign of liberation.'

I ask him why I have not so far heard clear views on the future of Canada.

'If you find us obtuse, it is because you in Quebec are not quite sure of what you want.' Touché!

'Is the West as separatist as I think?'

'Yes, and it has become more so in recent years. Mr. Lesage's journey out west did not help to clear the atmosphere.'

'Why?'

'Because he talked over the heads of his audience. Quebec should send a troup of missionaries across Canada', states Pierre Berton, 'to educate us on Quebec. Your public relations with the rest of this country are non-existent. No one really knows you, nor are we aware of what you are trying to accomplish. If the general attitudes of English Canadians could change toward Quebec, your people, I think, would be less demanding.'

'But how do you change the attitudes of people?'

'By having more people travel and work the way you do.'

'Why does English Canada hate us so much?'

'Because', slowly answers Pierre Berton, 'we are afraid of the unknown, because you know what you are, and we don't, and because you have an identity and some of us are still looking for one.'

5 p.m.
TORONTO

I am back at my hotel after having shopped at the bookstore, the grocer's, and other shops. Everywhere I spoke French, and everywhere I was met with courtesy and with a desire to help me. I feel comforted by this forgoing of the rude 'Speak

English' with which, years ago, I was told to use the other language of Canada.

I am ready to confess my admiration for the multitude of books on Canada by English-Canadian essayists, sociologists, historians, and professors. In French Canada, numerous books are published on our own social evolution, but we still lack observers able to study Canada with a national outlook. We should inquire more into the kind of turbulence caused in the rest of the country because of our social, political, and economic revolution. Before we declare Quebec an independent state, French Canadians should be fully aware of the implications stemming from such a break in our geographical and commercial territory.

I have often wondered why Nathan Cohen is considered the *bête noire* of English-Canadian theatre life. His harsh criticism is biting, but I know of no man in Canada who knows the substance of drama better. I owe him a debt of gratitude. Invited many times to take part on his 'Fighting Words', I have had the opportunity of meeting very alert Canadians. I write these lines with joy; if they are considered too personal, let my readers remember that this diary is intended to be personal.

'Don't forget, Solange,' grumbles my dear Nathan, 'we are a country formed by defeated nations. The French and the Americans defeated the English. The Scotch and the Irish were in turn beaten by the English, and you French Canadians have been conquered. Most of our immigrants also come from defeated countries.'

I told him how difficult it was to remain smiling when I was confronted with many clichés about Quebec.

'You will find fewer here. Toronto is changing every day,' he says. 'We are becoming a very cosmopolitan city.'

'So is Montreal, unfortunately. Only Quebec City seems to retain its full French flavour.'

'There is more anti-French feeling in Canada today. When the passions of nationalism are set in motion, nobody knows where they will stop. I do not fear a civil war in Quebec, but I am afraid of a recurrence of terrorism. Things are too quiet in

Quebec.' He draws a parallel between Quebec's terrorism and the Irish revolt in 1830 and comments on the Negro situation in the U.S.A.

'Look at the fight for civil rights. The more justice obtained by the Negro leaders, the more violent their youth become.'

Then he informs me that because he once suggested on his radio show that French TV shows should be broadcast on the English TV from eight to nine at night, he was deluged by hate literature from irate listeners who accused him of conniving with Quebec.

'Are there any solutions to our problems?'

'Yes, if we learn patience and if we project into a historical perspective our present actions. For example, who will remember in two generations the passions involved in adopting the maple leaf flag?'

Quebeckers will.

Monday, April 4
10 a.m.
TORONTO-LONDON
C.N.R.

Who in English Canada will sympathize with my frustrations when I try to send a telegram in French to my husband or my son? Of course, if I were to spend hours spelling each word over the telephone I might succeed, but my husband assures me that he also finds it frustrating to decipher this instant French.

Monday midnight
LONDON

I am less than three hours from Toronto, but nevertheless I feel as if I had gone back ten years in time. After the interesting hubbub of Toronto, London happily sleeps its richness away.

'The richest town per capita,' everyone repeats.

The University of Western Ontario, anachronistically draped

41

in Gothic hauteur, sticks out as a barren fortress of learning. Ronald Bates, professor of literature and one of the best critics of French-Canadian letters, receives me cordially and for hours we probe the soul of Quebec's poetry. I am amazed by the depth of his knowledge and by the quality of his admiration for our young generation of writers. But just before meeting his class, I am once again gripped with a bad case of stage fright. And why not? My young audience is polite, and politely bored. I do not sense any curiosity. They quietly voice their fear of bilingualism and they all are a little shocked to realize Quebec might disturb their pleasant way of life by demanding a special status in Confederation.

Later, I address Mason Wade's class and there I find more alertness to Quebec and Canada. But I am also distressed to discover that Mason Wade suspects every French Canadian who believes in independence of being close to lunacy. Maybe they are, but as André Laurendeau once wrote years ago, 'Some of us prefer lunacy to certain death.'

Once again I am confronted with the fact that the more I defend my separatist friends, the closer I come to their views. I simply cannot judge the separatists as crazy people obsessed with fantasy. I know many of them; they are as sincere and as honest with their hopes for Quebec as I hope I am.

Thursday, April 6
Noon
TORONTO
The Premier's Office
Parliament Buildings

For more than thirty minutes, Mr. Robarts has answered my questions frankly and with a great deal of self-assurance. In his presence, I suddenly realize that whoever he may be, the premier of Ontario carries much power in Canada. I am well acquainted with the British-turned-Canadian proverb 'East is east and west is west and never the twain shall meet,' but I maintain that if Western Canada were facing a break in Confederation, it would forget its differences with Ontario and follow Mr. Robarts's decisions either to support or to fight Quebec.

'Do you believe, Mr. Premier, that Ottawa is conceding to Quebec?'

'If Ottawa had, years ago, adopted a firm attitude, your demands would not appear as concessions. Ottawa is drifting into vague policies, and when it gives in to Quebec, its decision definitely looks like concession.'

'Do you think that French will ever become an official language in Ontario?'

'We are pragmatists here. My government has translation services to meet the demands of our Franco-Ontarians. Ontario is an English province and it will remain so. The day I were to force French on our population, I would greatly harm the position of French Canadians in Ontario. There still exists in Toronto some hard opposition to Quebec; it is better not to antagonize it openly, for although it is small, it is still very influential.'

'But if a premier of Ontario less sympathetic to Quebec should one day choose to cancel the right to French schools of your French population, one word would be sufficient. French Canadians have no rights in Ontario, they have only privileges.'

'This day will not come.'

'Will French Canadians ever achieve an equal status with your English-speaking population?'

'It is possible.'

'In Quebec we are under the impression that you understand us; but you seldom speak out. Why?'

'I am waiting for the findings of our Parliamentary Committee on Constitution to know exactly how I can support or fight Quebec's position.'

'Is your committee similar to ours?'

'Less partisan, I think. I don't even know what the political views are of some of the men I have appointed.'

'Do you believe that Quebec will become an independent state?'

His answer was blunt, hard, and very cold. 'No, this will not happen. I will not let it happen.'

I feel reassured, and at the same time afraid of the sudden power underlying his words.

'Will we see federal troops surrounding Quebec? Do you fear a civil war in Quebec?'

'Definitely not.'

I leave without exactly knowing whether Mr. Robarts is won over to us, or if he is calmly waiting for the right time to pounce on us.

April 8
10 a.m.
TORONTO-MONTREAL

Yesterday noon, I met Scott Symons, journalist, writer, and former curator of the Canadian museum of Ontario. He was one of the first English Canadians to foresee Quebec's quiet or unquiet revolution. After having lived for two years in Quebec, he still tries, sometimes with impatience, to understand our impatience. Today, totally absorbed in his writing, more like a character in his own novel than a novelist, he speaks violently and tries hard to use a truculent language to shock me. Not to disappoint him, I quickly rise to his baiting, but I am a bit bewildered by such unexpected anger. He throws his thoughts at me as one throws stones.

'I can't be fully happy in Ontario, but I can't live without Ontario.' 'English Canada stifles me but it also stifles French Canada.' 'Here in Toronto, we are half-dead bourgeois.'

Strangely, I found myself suddenly defending my Torontonian friends vehemently. He then informs me of his view of English Canada and of his prediction of the future.

'We will become a republic through our defeat, and we will lose much of what we thought was worth living for.'

Our conversation goes on and on, and I feel more and more depressed because there seems to be little hope for Canada, according to Scott Symons. Nevertheless, I am happy to have heard the opinions of an angry young English Canadian.

Hours later I meet another young writer, this time less violent, less exuberant, but more voluble.

'I see absolutely no use for Quebec in Confederation, except to maintain all of us in a united territory. You cannot be master in your house and remain in Canada.'

I am slowly and painfully beginning to believe him.

'The British North America Act is our spiritual country,' he suddenly says.

'As the Torah for the Jews.'

'Yes. We are sick of the small issues raised in Quebec; compared to what is going on in the world, it is worthless.'

So were the first troubles in Algeria, years ago.

2 p.m.
TORONTO-MONTREAL

My last evening in Toronto has been spent with Franco-Ontarians and Québécois. One phrase forms the motif of our discussion: 'Here we have no rights, only privileges. The Ontario government must change this situation.' Suddenly I remember a quotation from *The Artisan of the Middle Ages* by P. Shapiro: 'He had enough influence to voice his woe, but not enough to obtain justice.' Is this not the lot of the French-Canadian diaspora?

'We are more than six hundred thousand in Ontario; we are not a weak minority. But we should have more strength, more power, more influence. Some of us are afraid to speak out. We have left behind poor working conditions in Quebec; here our standard of living is higher and we are afraid that we will lose our jobs if we demand more rights in Ontario. Now and then we hear: "If you are not happy with what we give you here, go back to Quebec!" '

'You see, Madame Rolland,' explains an energetic French Canadian, 'if we do not want to be dispossessed here, we must always surpass ourselves.'

'Five years ago,' sighs a very timid young woman, 'if we spoke French in the buses, we were rudely told "Speak English, or leave the car." '

'And now?'

45

'Now things are better because Quebec is stronger. But when you Québécois speak angrily, we pay for it here. English Canadians are suddenly harder with us. Of course on the surface nothing ever shows, but our promotions are suddenly blocked, or slowed down. They are very cunning in their ways of dealing with us. It's hard to pin down their attitude precisely.'

'If only the English Catholic priests would help us. They are sometimes our worst enemies. When one realizes what is going on in the Irish Catholic milieu, it is a wonder that anyone still remains a good Catholic,' proffers a very bitter businessman.

'How can we have a chance in life, madame?' asks another. 'We pay a heavy price for retaining our French identity. My son studies French from Grade 1 to Grade 3. Then he goes to a bilingual school, and in his eighth grade he learns English only. If I am rich enough I will send him to a Quebec university, and there again he will be handicapped.'

'Why then do you wish to retain your French identity?' I inquired.

'I don't know any more,' admits the father.

'But I know,' retorts my young French-Canadian friend. 'I was born French and I am going to die a French Canadian. If I cannot do it here, then I will go back to Quebec.'

I am an outsider in their midst. I feel spoiled, wealthy. My life in Quebec is easy; theirs in Ontario is complicated. But I understand their feelings. If I were to live outside Quebec, I too would form a 'resistance', and I would let no one deprive me of my French identity. Suddenly a concrete idea comes to me: 'The answer to some of your problems lies in the strength of your protests against all infringement of your constitutional rights. For more than fifty years, everywhere in this country, French Canadians have been fighting for survival; but your struggles are isolated, lost in the vast Canadian design. Stand up together from coast to coast, and create right now a National Federation of the French Canadian Minorities. Your needs are all the same but the ways to achieve them differ from one province to the other. When your cry for justice is voiced by 800,000 individuals, the government will listen to you. You will become an electoral risk and we all know to what extent our noble politicians will stoop to get a vote!'

46

I shock them a little bit; they fear any drastic action; but by and by my enthusiasm reaches them. French Canada does not exist outside Quebec; tonight, in this lonely hotel room, we are trying to give it a bold new structure.

April 15
LAC MAROIS
La Cédraie

Montreal is definitely not a separatist town, but many Montrealers are separatists. Toronto is not anti-Quebec, but some Torontonians are 'fed up with French Canada'.

I have forgotten to note that during my euphoric stay in Toronto I was brought down to earth by an article in the *Telegram*, titled 'Either shut up or get out'. In other words, accept what English Canada decides for you, or get out of Canada. Those of us who are not separatists will become so, simply to offset such harsh words. A cab driver told me the same thing:

'You are a French Canadian.'

'Yes, and you?'

'A Hungarian.'

'Are you happy in Toronto?'

'In Toronto, only Torontonians are accepted. As for you, lady, you are considered a foreigner here just like me.'

A stranger in my own land . . . and in Toronto too! *Quelle tristesse!*

I am asked by a journalist to define an English Canadian's outlook. I must weigh my answer. 'The French struggle to retain their identity and the non-French are looking for one,' states John Porter in his brilliant book *The Vertical Mosaic*. I am in accord with this observation. An English Canadian is an individual in search of his soul, passionately attached to traditions in which he does not recognize himself. Between an English Canadian of 1966 and an Englishman there is no common ground. The world looks to London for excitement, not to Toronto or Vancouver. An English Canadian is a man comfortably living in a present he no longer understands, a man frightened by the independence of his country who instinctively looks toward another nation for strength. He is a gardener enamoured of a rose, timid with a woman, respectful of a land he would rather look at than live in. He is a puritan in his responses but a rabelaisian when alcohol loosens his heart and his mind. He is a poet who hides in poetry, a citizen sure of his rights, a biblical builder by his Scottish descent. He is someone who reaches into the past to justify his future. He is a discreet and eminently loyal friend. He is a person in search of himself but afraid of the self he may find.

And if, reading these lines, someone tells me I do not understand the English Canadian, I will readily accept this judgment.

April 25
LAC MAROIS
La Cédraie

Around me, open suitcases, dresses and suits piled on the beds. My son, sad because his mother has been transformed into a nomad, suddenly wonders: 'Maman, do you think people out west will listen to you?' No, they will not, and I feel oppressed, sad, a little afraid of this journey.

Since my return from Toronto fifteen days ago, tension has mounted in me. My French-Canadian friends are impatient with me. 'You can keep your English Canadians,' they say. 'We are fed up with them.'

A friend of mine whose mature judgment has always calmed my anger is now turning into a fierce separatist. Obliged to be part of a crew of TV journalists and cameramen from Toronto, she was treated with paternalism and with the 'big brother attitude'.

'I have been on television longer than most of these English Canadians, and for one solid week, they advised me on how to do my job,' she fumed.

This is a steady pattern of behaviour between French and English Canadians. Without realizing it, English Canadians take over, and invariably tell us how to act, think, and speak. Today

I refuse to take part in any bilingual or national association because I resent automatically being asked to translate the immortal words of my English colleagues sitting on the same committee.

EN ROUTE FOR
BRITISH COLUMBIA

*Where your treasury is,
there your heart is also.*

W. A. C. Bennett

Twelve hours aboard this train and the scenery has still not changed. Birches, pines, cedars, frozen lakes disappear behind as my train runs for the Pacific sun. This never-ending voyage permits me to appreciate the vastness of Canada.

I leave my itinerant bedroom at seven p.m. to sit in the bar. A traveller from North Bay recognizes me and opens a conversation. We are both enjoying our martinis, and we discuss the different laws on alcohol in different provinces.

'Sunday', he warns me, 'this train will be dry.'

'I know, and my husband has offered me a portable bar.'

'Your husband is not afraid of the W.C.T.U.?' he asked.

'What on earth is this?'

'It is the Women's Christian Temperance Union.'

'It sounds menacing.'

'It is.' He went on to tell me that in his youth it was customary to say, 'Lips that touch wine shall never touch mine.'

'Are you the lady who is writing a book on Canada?' inquires a sailor.

'Yes.'

'Take care what you say about us, lady, for we English are just about to fix you.'

Bon. I will.

'I'll be honest with you, madame,' said an officer. 'How can you expect us to feel at home in Quebec when so few speak our language?'

Who is aware that I must forget *my* language in nine provinces?

'It is our Church-ridden spirit that ties us down,' confesses a French Canadian residing in Peace River. 'I am not anti-clerical, but often our curates do not permit us to live freely. In one generation, there will probably be no French Canadians out west. We should unite to form a close group, madame.'

'Why not create one strong French newspaper for Western Canada, instead of publishing three or four small and weak ones?' I asked.

'You are right, our newspaper should publish national news, not only parochial gossip. We are 50,000 in Alberta and *La Survivance* has about 300 readers.'

'Why?'

'Because the newspaper is uninteresting. It's too local, too much under the wing of the Church. Here we are still living on chaplains' time.'

Everywhere in Canada so far, young French Canadians have told me how grateful they are to their clergy but how fed up with being trapped by too much clericalism.

'What do most French Canadians in Western Canada think about the situation in Quebec?'

'Some of our leaders are denouncing you as atheists, and they pretend that soon you will take all religion away from your schools.'

I protest. Between raising the quality of Quebec's education and taking religion out of schools built to meet the demands of a Catholic population, there is a great difference. Our population would never tolerate a secular system of education void of spiritual values.

Since we left Winnipeg, I have discovered the prairies. Suddenly I feel like a character out of *Doctor Zhivago*. Like the Russian heroes, I am searching for a mystique; I am seeking the soul of my country. I too am lost on a deserted plain. Mine, rich with wheat, speaks of appeased hunger. My thoughts are far from Quebec; they are centred on India and on its hunger. Why is there so much wheat here for such a small population and so little rice there for millions? The hunger commandos have not yet found their universal store-houses.

'Do you speak Parisian French or Quebec French?'

How can the English Canadians be convinced of their utter ridiculousness when, unable to say one decent word of French, they come out with such a stupid question? Educated people have always known that the worst French spoken in France usually comes from Paris. Not all Parisians are guilty of such a crime against phonetics, but Parisian French has always been met with jests.

'Non, monsieur, I definitely and proudly do not speak Parisian French. I try to speak international French with, of course, a Quebec accent. Do you speak London English?'

'No,' he says introducing his daughter to me. She greets me with the polite and ubiquitous expression, 'Hi.'

Shakespeare would have shuddered! I do too.

3 p.m.
EDMONTON-JASPER

The Winnipeg *Free Press* is reproducing an article by Charles Lynch on the Commission on Bilingualism and Biculturalism. I have seldom read lines as childish as these. Mr. Lynch writes: 'I thought the Commission's report would hurt rather than help the cause of national unity.' These words stem from his anger because one researcher asked for his views on Quebec, on his French friends, etc.

His opinions remind me that so far I have not written a word on the Laurendeau-Dunton commission. It is definitely not easy for me to speak about it. Furthermore, I am fiercely proud of my complete independence from it. I have never written a brief or been asked to submit ideas. From time to time, I have met one or two commissioners attending the same seminars. We have discussed bilingualism and biculturalism, but I have never asked for a precise opinion. It would have been indiscreet of me to seek one, since I am to write about Canada as an individual, not as part of any federal or provincial institution.

Since the publication of the Preliminary Report, English Canada is obliged to realize that its secret animosity toward Quebec is now in the public square. As a result, the English Canadian sees himself as we have seen him for two hundred years, and because he is honest, he does not like what he sees. But instead of accepting his prejudices, he prefers to accuse the Royal Commission of being 'out to break the country'. As if the country had not been broken long before any politician dreamed of such a commission! Surely the Royal Commission must not be considered infallible. I frankly despise the kind of questions their researchers ask. I would refuse to answer any of them, but does that turn the whole commission into a malevolent group eager to break a country that they are, in fact, hoping to save?

This is a difficult, segregated, regionalized country; people living in it bear no love for each other. Why then should we think that the solution to our national sickness will be easy and agreeable? French Canada does not put all its trust in the Royal Commission on Bilingualism and Biculturalism, but most of our leaders have the decency to wait until the last Report is published before they praise or condemn the Laurendeau-Dunton commission. Why can't English Canada do the same?

My train is skirting Mount Bonhomme and Grisette. Surely one of my ancestors passed through here centuries ago.

The kindness of the staff aboard the train has not been simply because I was recommended to them by the railway's directors. It has been a spontaneous expression of interest in this diary. Because they had seen me work every day, the cook, the conductor, the barman, the waiters, the porters came this morning to say good-bye, and they all promised to read my book. I have learned more from them than from some passengers.

Today I live in a Dufy décor, against a background of sailboats, mountains covered with snow, sea-gulls, and tug-boats. I am far from my French environment, and I am dazed by the beauty and the flowers. Here, so far, I have discovered no animosity but a jaunty indifference toward French Canada, who would 'never dare leave Confederation'.

'We don't mind Quebec, but Ontario, yes.' Why this hatred for Bay Street?

'Our cars cost a lot more here than they do down east. How simple for us to buy them in Seattle or Washington, or San Francisco.'

How simple, yes. But how Americanized can economy become?

The editor of the *Province* has widened my knowledge of British Columbia, for I have learned that the population in B.C. is largely ignorant of the Quebec situation.

'We hear about it, we read about it, but it never has a real impact on us.' Paddy Sherman speaks of British Columbia in terms of 'this country'. I then draw a parallel between the needs of Quebec and the demands of Premier W. A. C. Bennett on Ottawa.

Paddy Sherman replies, 'We need more power of taxation; we are also trying to open a free zone of exchange between the U.S.A. and B.C. If the barriers created to protect Eastern Canada from American prices were ever removed, our standard of living would rise. Bennett has often compared B.C. to a cow fed here and milked in Ottawa.'

'Is B.C. separatist?'

'No. There is no question of our leaving Canada, but if the political situation became too tense, we might seek the status of a dominion allied with the British Commonwealth. We owe

56

nothing to the rest of Canada. Our population comes chiefly from England, the United States, and European countries. We are pragmatists here; we seldom ask why we must do this or that, but *how* we can do it. In the light of this attitude the recent tour of Premier Lesage has greatly disappointed his audience.'

'Did he speak over the heads of his listeners?'

'No. He simply bored us. He was too vague about what Quebec wants and how she can achieve her aims. But his honesty and his sincerity greatly impressed us.'

British Columbians do not resent concessions to Quebec, but they are much more sensitive to the problems of bilingualism and biculturalism within their own province.

'We joined Canada in 1871,' Paddy Sherman continues. 'The idea of two founding races has no meaning in B.C. We are fully conscious of the obligation to learn a second language. But why French, since this language is used less in B.C.?'

'You are British Columbians first, then.'

'Every province is the same,' observes Sherman. 'We become real Canadians in times of crisis, during a war or to offset an economic recession. Then we wake up to our Canadian identity. Here we lead a privileged life; we are able to golf, ski, sail, climb mountains, garden, ten months every year. Philosophical discussion is not popular in B.C.'

May 4
10 a.m.
VANCOUVER

Every day I meet people with differing attitudes. A young mother tells me of her desperate efforts to learn French. But she adds, 'When we ask for more hours of conversational French in our schools, we are usually asked in turn, "Why do you want your children to learn French? Will it make them better doctors or engineers?" '

'Down east', as everyone says here, we are a little too quick to judge British Columbia as a separatist province. I have found no trace of this tendency here, but I have discovered a sense of isolationism. Distance is a psychological factor: why complicate life with problems confronting people three thousand miles away?

I marvel at everyone's amiability. If I seem lost, many people offer to help me, and in French, too. I am not obliged to force people to talk about B.C. Here they all seemed mesmerized by the view, the sun, and the flowers. Everyone is proud of his province and of the way Mr. Bennett manages its rich land. But except for one or two intellectuals and journalists, so far no one has asked questions about Quebec. I did not expect this charming, polite, and friendly indifference to us.

For the Franco-Columbians, the political situation in B.C. is unique. No law decrees French an illegal language. After having been one of the languages of education between 1793 and 1850, French has lost its rights because, recalls Roméo Paquette, leader of the French community, 'slowly and surely we were displaced by the gold rush, and the English and American immigrants. In the next generation you will find it hard to discover one real British Columbian. Two-thirds of our population is heterogeneous.'

'How many French Canadians live in B.C.?'

'There were 66,960 French Canadians living in British Columbia in 1964, but 61.4 per cent have been assimilated.'

'Why?'

'Because we have privileges granted to us only by the goodwill of the people. We have no political, ethnic, or civil structures. Our bilingual schools have no precise programs in French. The French sisters teach in English; they submit to pressure. Thus French gradually loses its importance. Here, one system of education has been set up for everyone. We live here through the tolerance of British Columbians; we are a thorn in their flesh.'

'Are there any solutions to your problems?'

'It would be foolish for us to think that one day we might be considered as full citizens with our own rights; we are immigrants as all the others. We must not therefore seek to transform public opinion, but we should interpose between English

58

Canadians and ourselves a system of education adapted to our own specific needs. I am happy to report that soon we will have a French public school completely supported by the provincial government. British Columbia will be the most progressive province in Canada in regard to its French minorities.'

His pride is quite moving. It could not have been easy to convince not only the political authorities of B.C. but also the French-Canadian Catholics of the necessity for these public schools.

'One of our priests said, "All I ask of these schools is that they maintain a Christian attitude," ' relates Mr. Paquette.

'A bishop went as far as to say: "There are two issues to consider: the French public school which is a privilege, and the French Catholic school which is an ideal. We must not refuse the privilege for the sake of the ideal." '

I hope such a mature outlook on the education of minorities will be adopted by all provinces. The sooner we realize that public schools are the answer to the complex system of education in Canada, the better the position of French and English will be.

May 9
VANCOUVER

My husband, André, arrived yesterday from Montreal and brought me some newspapers and news of the children. Somehow British Columbia feels a bit like home. With him, I live at least a few hours a day in French.

A recent lunch, given for me by professors at the University of British Columbia, comforts me. The deans of art, of law, and of history are deeply interested in the social revolution in Quebec and their keen questions bring me out of my complete sense of isolation. I love these long and unprepared discussions; they encourage a frank exchange of ideas between people. In general, Canada's avant-garde political thinkers come from an academic milieu; it is essential that our government call on more professors, more intellectuals, to ferment our ideas. Here, as in other parts of Canada, a cleavage exists between the policy of

59

the provincial government and the universities. Listening to deans Soward, Curtis, and Healy, and speaking with many other professors, I soon discover a similarity between their Mr. Bennett and our Mr. Duplessis. The infamous 'toi tais-toi' of the late premier of Quebec is echoed by Mr. Bennett's 'You don't have to answer this' yelled at Health Minister Eric Martin. Though the intellectuals deplore Mr. Bennett's attitude, they all agree on his sincerity, his honesty, and his loyalty to British Columbia. Ottawa's centralizing policy is not well looked upon in B.C., and I feel, because of this attitude, very much at ease in explaining Quebec's position.

I had dinner with some good friends a few days ago, and they all were curious about Quebec. What a relief! But during the evening I stumbled onto an argument which has always angered me: 'When I go to Quebec,' said a businessman, 'why am I obliged to speak French?'

'In a province in which eighty per cent of our population is of French origin, it is perfectly normal to express ourselves in French, twenty-four hours a day,' I stated impatiently. His 'perhaps' irritated me. If a French Canadian is not allowed to live like a French Canadian in Quebec, where else can we go to remain true to ourselves? I cannot understand the average English Canadian who seems literally terrified at the idea of saying one or two words in French. I like to quote the exasperated exclamation of a famous British sociologist attending the 1965 conference at Couchiching: 'What's the matter with you English Canadians?' he asked. 'You all act as if it were a sin to speak French.'

I am able to discuss the constitutional or political aims of Quebec calmly, but when I am forced to remind my interlocutors of the democratic rights of French Canadians in their own province, I lose my patience. The average English Canadian never misses an occasion to remind French Canadians of his respect for individual rights, but if these individuals' rights are French, he could not care less. So far, I have never met a single English Canadian, intellectual, politician, or journalist, who has loyally accepted his wrongs *vis-à-vis* the French minorities of his own province. The fate of French Canadians living in English

Canada seems perfectly normal to most English Canadians.

Everywhere I have travelled, I have spoken to hundreds of French Canadians, alert, intelligent, eager to discuss their problems, but here, as in Toronto, I have been asked by most British Columbians, 'Where are those French Canadians? We never meet them anywhere.' Even if I were to write pages and pages on the global indifference of English toward French Canadians, I would surely be told, 'Down east they are like this,' or 'Out west they may act this way, but not here.' And if I remind an English Canadian of his friendship, of his eagerness to talk with me, invariably he will answer: 'But that is different – you are not the same.'

In what do I differ from my French-speaking compatriot? If my difference comes from the fact that through God's grace I am 'living on the side of the world that does not know hunger',* then, yes, I do differ from some of my compatriots. But as one who is becoming more and more a Québécoise first and Canadienne second, I am the same as all of us. I am proud of my nationality and I rise up in anger whenever I discover contempt for it. This is why British Columbia, in spite of its beauty, its flowers, its glorious spring, can never be my country. So far I have not met animosity; but the smiling pragmatism of the British Columbian is contrary to my aim as a writer, as a human being. I live here in low gear and it would take little to lure me to this *dolce vita*, which I resent so much. I listen to my new friends speak of Canadianism and I cannot reconcile their patriotism with their attitude that the crisis of Canada is a 'problem for Quebec and Ottawa, not for us'. Ontario and Bay Street are the enemies of this easy and peaceful existence. I could not write or live in such a tranquil atmosphere. I need more passion around me, more quest for truth, more desire to become a better human being.

I will always remember everyone's kindness to me, everyone's immediate friendship. Surrounded by such kindness, I nearly forgot my difficult mission!

'Why don't you enjoy life instead of working?' I was asked.

'I do enjoy life, but my kind of French life'.

*Jean Guéhenno, *La Foi difficile*.

Nothing in this country seems adjusted to a human scale. I spoke in English at noon in Qualicum Beach, this afternoon in French in Victoria. I am slightly dazed by this difficult exercise in bilingualism and biculturalism. If I think of my audiences' reactions, I could pretend that all is well in Canada.

'We practise an egalitarian policy here,' affirms Robert Bonner, 'we treat all Canadians with equality.' For him the concept of two nations in Canada will never be valid.

'Put your faith in the Canadian's good sense,' he advises. The problems of Canada are 'blown out of proportion' by journalists, politicians, and 'you people', and he goes on to say that he doesn't at all believe in the possibility of the independence of Quebec. 'Canadians are much too sensible to allow such a thing.' He answers slowly when I ask him if, in the event of a secession by Quebec, Canada would join the United States.

'If the United States should accept us as their new State, they would do so on certain conditions and in accepting these, we would have to crawl on our knees. Canadians are a proud nation,' he states.

Proud of what, and because of what? But I dare not voice my question. I leave his office rather bewildered by his smiling conviction in a melting-pot version of Canada.

'We are all Canadians and we must remain so,' he reiterated.

In turn I reiterate my question. What kind of Canadians? English only?

Last night I was received with cordiality by Bruce Hutchison, journalist, author, and publisher of the Vancouver *Sun*. I spent an hour in his charming Elizabethan house.

'It will take time to change the attitudes of Canadians. For centuries we have lived in the tranquil and comforting assurance that Quebec was a quaint province, inhabited by lumbermen content to live poor but happy. Suddenly, without warning, Quebec announces its intention to lead Canada in a new concept of Canadianism. Naturally our reaction has been strong, and because we are not ready to revise our vision of peaceful democracy, we have hardened ourselves against you.' He continues to have faith in Canada's future because he had expected a more violent reaction from English Canada. With me, Bruce Hutchison hopes that John Robarts might lead the other provinces into a possible compromise with Quebec. He admits that British Columbia is far removed from Ottawa, but realizes that Canadian problems concern the entire nation, not only Ottawa and Quebec.

And for a short time we open a frank dialogue on all aspects of federalism and provincialism. Because I am more than worried with the objectivity of my diary, I quote some passages to him and inquire whether he thinks I have been too personal, too emotional.

'Be as personal, as emotional as you want to be. Don't let anyone tell you what to say or not to say. This country needs a book like yours – we are fed up with experts.'

May 10
VICTORIA–VANCOUVER
Aboard the S.S. 'Royal Victorian'

My thoughts this morning are straying to the Greek Islands. I am haunted by my memory of them. The sea, here too, is studded with small islands. Against a blue sky the Maple Leaf ripples. For the first time, this flag suddenly looks to me young, gay, *dans le vent*. I am refreshed by these peaceful hours on the enchanting Pacific Ocean.

May 12
PRINCE RUPERT

André comes back smiling from this strange little town located on the frontier of Alaska, because yesterday afternoon he caught a salmon, as big as that!

'Fishing', he declares seriously, 'is the best way to unite Canadians.'

63

I never thought of this!

Guests of a paper company, we are received with kindness, warmth, and a little curiosity. The first night, we meet everyone in Prince Rupert at a reception given for us. I hear many opinions on Quebec and Canada.

'Quebec spells romance,' dreams a young woman.

'We hate Ontario, but we would love to know Quebec better,' states a businessman.

'I would not mind at all joining the United States. What difference would it make?' someone else remarks.

'The Americans will not hurt us,' continues another. 'I see no reason to fear them.'

'Your system of education is no good; you have been educated to become priests, nuns, or lawyers, not to be good businessmen.'

Will I ever forget my husband's face?

May 14
PRINCE RUPERT—VANCOUVER
Flight 6

Will Hankinson, director of CBC, opens my eyes to British Columbia's resentment. 'Here one often hears the expression, "If you had lived with those dirty frogs during the war, you would hate them as I do." '

In B.C., the CBC is going to broadcast in French on an FM network.

'Now Ottawa wants to impose French culture on our way of life,' wrote most of the Vancouver newspapers.

'This is a good but costly experiment,' complained most French Canadians. 'We are not rich and we will have to spend at least fifty dollars to buy an FM radio.'

I pass signs pointing to Slumber Lodge, Pondorosa Units, Shangrila Grill, Riviera-on-Mountain, Hi-way Motel. We too have our Jeanne D'Arc Valet Service, Saint-Joseph-Barbecue. How elegant can we English and French be?

We live in a country in which there is everything to see; practically nothing to visit.

Some women have inherited from God a certain graciousness. In Vancouver, I was received by Madame Ethel Wilson, 'one of the best novelists of Canada', Gwethalyn Graham had said. What a charming visit this was! We conversed in French, in a French infinitely purer than the infamous Parisian French, and Madame Wilson seemed happy with my Quebec French.

Where is the panoramic vision and spirit of our ancestors who built against perilous odds a railway to unite this country? Canadians paid a fortune for this steel link, but once the railway was finished they sat on each side of the tracks and were content to watch the trains going by.

Two hours of flying and five hundred miles later, we arrive in Banff. I write my diary in front of a large window overlooking a breath-taking view. The mountain peaks, white against a blue sky, invite me outdoors, but unfortunately the Centennial and my editors have an urgency that my reason must accept. So back to work it is.

I have learned a great deal from my visit in British Columbia. If I lived in this flowering province, the Riviera of Canada, if my education had been pragmatist and practical, I too would probably feel quite detached about the Canadian problems. But it is impossible in 1966 to ignore the soul of this nation.

ALBERTA

*"It is better to live rich,
than to die rich."*
James Boswell

Calgary is a rich town, divided between financiers, oil-men, and ranchers. Here there is supposed to exist a deep, cold, and furious hardening against Quebec. But for twenty-four hours, I have found myself in a very French and very Calgarian atmosphere, because Gertrude Laing, the only woman on the Laurendeau-Dunton commission, lives here. Therefore, Calgary appears friendly and less difficult to conquer.

I do not know the Calgarians' attitude towards Madame Laing, but Western Canada should be very proud to be represented, on one of the most important Royal Commissions ever created in Canada, by someone for whom bilingualism and biculturalism is not a temporary interest but an experience fully lived for many years.

Westerners are prone to repeat that Quebec wants to run the country. Yesterday I was asked to comment on this assumption. If Quebec wanted to dominate Canada, I would be the first to underline the clumsiness of our leaders on the federal scene. They have allowed too many scandals affecting the political careers of French Canadians to blur the image of Quebec.

But there is a difference, difficult for Westerners to accept, between Quebec's reputed desire to run the country and its genuine wish to have a stronger voice in the policy of the country. During elections, the Quebecker's vote usually supports the party most aware of his needs, and Quebec may place its trust in a prime minister who many times is unable to gather such influential support from the other provinces. Thus it becomes easy to believe that Quebec controls Parliament. In general, the average English Canadian never bothers to analyse Quebec's vote seriously. He judges quickly the result of any election and then repeats clichés without fully realizing he has invented them to suit his moods.

No, Quebec does not want to lead or to run Canada, but our state, different, distinctive, given special privileges by the British North America Act, thinks that the time is ripe for the rest of this country to share with us the decisions determining our Canadian destiny. We believe it would be beneficial to Canada if our French way of thinking could influence our international and national policy. Therefore, through constitutional amendments and democratic pressures, we seek a stronger partnership with English Canada.

I am having lunch with Donald Gordon, once attached to the CBC as its London representative and now teaching in Calgary at the University of Alberta. He greets me with six copies of *Le Devoir*, and I am so excited by this unexpected confrontation with my French life that spontaneously I give him my trust and my friendship. We talk for hours on subjects as varied as Calgary life and the troubles of 'This Hour Has Seven Days'.

'Our youth is standing up to the demands of our present. The young generation is exasperated with the clumsiness of our government and it is searching for a new identity. Here our society is fragmented; it is still a society without traditions, without roots. In 1940, Calgary had 60,000 citizens; today, we are more than 250,000. The present generation is in transition; we are still deeply concerned with the survival of the fittest.'

'Here we live in harmony, in peace,' affirms a French Canadian born in Edmonton, 'and the disturbances in Quebec infringe on our tranquillity. We read the newspapers, watch television, but we are not deeply concerned with Quebec.'

I wonder then why those of the French-Canadian diaspora resent our complacency toward them.

'We have founded a French kindergarten,' continues a French-Canadian housewife. 'We have no real teachers but our classes have met with great success.'

Everywhere in Canada, and here in Alberta particularly, I have noticed a renewal of interest in bilingualism, but always it is the French Canadians who, under tremendous difficulty and at great personal cost, are responsible for maintaining French as a living language. They are to be commended for their devotion.

Everywhere in Canada, it is the same ugly story, the same failure to respect the fundamental rights of citizens to be educated in one of the official languages of this country. I would never impose French on anyone, but I cannot accept that French Canadians living in Eastern or Western Canada are not allowed to remain true to their identity in a country which prides itself on having fought wars to permit other nations to retain their identity. I am at times like these ashamed of my country.

May 19
11.00 a.m.
CALGARY

This morning I have to confess my complete intellectual exhaustion. For twenty days, I have spoken, written, discussed, argued in English only and I am now empty of words. No one seems to understand why I suddenly fumble with every sentence. At the end of a long day of discussion, in English only, on the advantages of bilingualism, I have great difficulty resisting the urge to throw my glass up in the air when one of my guests remarks lightly. 'Oh, let's all be Canadians.'

I shall carry back with me from Calgary a wide range of opinions. When I arrived here, I did not know much about this ebullient town. I know less upon departing. It is difficult to crystallize my thoughts on anything precise, and somehow I am always on the defensive. Everyone is more than friendly, eager to talk with me, but no one agrees with one another. I am bewildered by this harvest of views on government policy, education, bilingualism, and anti-Semitism ('which exists in Alberta', affirms a Jewish businessman).

'This is a man's world; Calgary is a masculine city,' I am told. Maybe this is why the refined elegance of the women of Calgary is so striking. They have to prove themselves, I am told, and they choose a lovely way to do it.

'Our leaders still consider cultural and intellectual activities as feminine pastimes. Our society is therefore materialistic and anti-cultural. Art is flourishing in Calgary, but not openly,' regrets a woman involved in social work. 'Sensitivity is not the first quality of our milieu.'

No one, except journalists, questions me on Quebec, but nearly everyone I have interviewed has told me what we are supposed to want, and what we will not get!

'You want too much for yourself and you give nothing to others.'

'You have nothing to offer us anyway,' objects a businessman.

'Do not be surprised to discover a great deal of animosity toward Quebec,' some professors advise me. No, I am not surprised; just a little fed up, and a little lonelier.

The Calgarian does not impress me as having a fond feeling for his neighbours. 'Vancouver? A land of lotus-eaters,' he says with contempt, and his 'down east' is articulated with a false sense of superiority.

'Here we stand for free enterprise,' an industrialist affirms loudly and he reiterates this fact with such masculine authority that I dare not disagree with him. Such virility is indeed a little oppressive!

71

'We are rejected as a group,' complains a Franco-Albertan, 'but not as individuals.' He expresses my inner thoughts well. I, too, am accepted as an individual; a spontaneous current of sympathy flows between my new friends and me. But when I speak as a French Canadian, or when I say 'Quebec wants', or 'Quebec will do this or that', immediately I detect a barrier. Faces close, smiles disappear, cordiality freezes. Many people have showered me with affection but they cannot understand why I resent so much their attitude toward my people, my province, my identity. It is absolutely futile to hope that one day a French Canadian will be a full citizen in Western Canada. He will always remain an immigrant, *comme les autres*.

Why hang on to a Confederation which has succeeded in kindling such animosity, such jealousy, such misunderstandings between the provinces? Do the people of France despise each other with such gusto? When a Frenchman talks about Angoulême, he feels like singing; when a Parisian remembers La Bourgogne, his mouth waters. Here, it is a common practice to hear one province attack another. I do not react as a French Canadian to this national pettiness but as a human being drained of love, of affection, of mutual respect. People speak to me with frankness, with spontaneity, but they all advise me not to judge English Canada on 'your impressions of Vancouver or Victoria. British Columbia is a selfish province only concerned with its own needs. Alberta is more open than Ontario, and do not forget that in the Maritimes we Westerners are as much strangers as you are.'

I am baffled by the evident contradiction of those who affirm loudly 'Let's all be Canadians' and spend most of their time criticizing other Canadians. To be a 'Canadian first' does not mean to be united to serve Canada's interest, but to say 'zut' to Quebec!

If Quebec's weaknesses lie in its education, on what rests English Canada's weak sense of identity? If the English-Canadian system of education were much better than Quebec's, as it is claimed, Canadian literature would speak of a strong nation instead of profiling a schizophrenic people. I accept the undemocratic aspect of our past education, but I find it rather startling to note that almost everywhere in Canada, taxi drivers, bartenders, simple people invariably tell me, 'I don't know why these fellows [the French Canadians] don't get their schools if they want them,' while politicians, intellectuals, writers do their utmost to deprive my French compatriots of their rights.

May 22
EDMONTON

Father Pâtoine, Louis Desrochers, and Professor Roger Motut, leaders of the Franco-Albertan community, are hopeful and full of projects for their compatriots. In Edmonton, the French-Canadian situation has greatly improved in recent years. After many years of discussions they have obtained better bilingual schools, and they reject my theory that public schools are the answer to the problems of the French minorities: 'Religion is our protection against sure assimilation.'

While I torture myself to come up with some bold ideas to alleviate our national difficulties, I learn of the refusal of L'Union Général des Etudiants du Québec to take part officially in a project sponsored by the students of the University of Alberta to celebrate Confederation. David Estrin, founder of the French Week in Edmonton in which I took part two years ago, informs me: 'The Week of the Second Century is a project suggested by students of Canadian universities. Students from all over Canada will meet to inform the citizens of Canada of the role, the life, the activities of students of Canada.'

L'Union will not take part in this project because they reject all Centennial celebrations. Because I am no longer twenty, I have lost patience with their childish tantrums. The students from Montreal, Sherbrooke, and Laval are in majority separatists, and this is within their rights. Their sincerity, their devotion to Quebec, their efforts to acquire high standards of education are widely known and admired in Quebec. I am fully conscious of their seriousness and their concern for politics, but why on earth are they so pretentious? Their refusal to mix with students of other provinces, their lack of courtesy in not inviting

73

them to their campuses, are forms of narcissism, and one day they will find themselves alone, and alone in admiring each other. To refuse to participate in the life of a community, to pretend we are the only individuals in Canada aspiring to better democracy and social reforms is a ridiculous assumption. We are justified in our protest when other provinces in Canada deny our French-speaking compatriots the right to live as they want; why then should we allow ourselves the same intolerance? I too think it is rather foolish to imagine that because we are going to sing 'O Canada' for 365 days in 1967, we will, the next year, all become big loving brothers; but I cannot understand what Quebec will gain by letting hotheads ruin the plan for a Centennial year of celebration.

I find myself torn by a strange paradox: this trip, this diary, has been made possible because of a Centennial grant, yet the more I visit in Canada, the less reason I find to celebrate a hundred years of living together. Even if Quebec were to secede from Canada, can we honestly assume that our surroundings will become automatically French, or that we can survive in splendid French isolation? Today we retain the power to decree French as the first language of Quebec, but tomorrow who will oblige Americans and English Canadians to use our language in their business transactions with us? Though we may be independent and free to live in French among ourselves, in fifty years we will have to master English to live in an enclave surrounded by 250 million English-speaking neighbours! Isolated on an English-American-Spanish continent, we will be ignored by the world if we maintain our tradition of living within our close-knit community.

May 23
EDMONTON

Eli Mandel, poet, writer, and critic, has praised our young French-Canadian poets. Because of his culture and the scope of his knowledge of Quebec's literature, I am able to talk to him without being obliged to write a detailed list of our writers and artists' names.

74

The road is never-ending and deserted. We are in the heart of the prairie solitude. In the distance, one or two houses stand close together. Here nature resembles the paintings of our remarkable Jean-Paul Lemieux. This great artist has not only captured the mood of our vast land, but has penetrated the core of Canadian loneliness.

SASKATCHEWAN

*This dominion which has
started in Lamentations
may end in Exodus.*
Sir Richard Cartwright

Since Calgary, I have discovered a world completely influenced by the skies; if the land is somewhat similar from one town to another, the skies are poignant with ever-changing colours from dawn to dusk. The farmers are conditioned by a dark or a light sky; as our fishermen in Gaspé are always looking out to sea to foretell their luck, the farmers look to the sky to guess whether it will rain, whether their harvest will be rich or poor. Nature plays an important role in forming our character and it would be unfair to judge the Westerners without taking into consideration the geographic milieu in which they live, work, and die.

May 24
SASKATOON
Mystica Farm

We have passed an enchanting day on a farm approximately six miles from Saskatoon. Guests of the writer Jim Wright and his wife, we have listened to tales of the prairies. Jim Wright loves his land and he talks abundantly about the farmers and their hardships. In one of his books, I discover the attractive character Louise Lucas, 'mother of the CCF', as they call her in Saskatchewan. Western television should be wise enough to adapt her life to the screen. Her story would make a wonderful series, authentically Canadian rather than imported from Texas or Oregon. We Eastern Canadians have no idea of life on the prairies; we often speak of rich ranchers sipping mint julep beside an oil well. Their daily routines are hard, difficult.

We spoke little of Quebec. I have so much to learn from these exchanges of views with people not afraid to voice their love for their native land.

SASKATOON
Radio Station CFNS

'Day by day, month by month, we are losing our desire to fight,' confesses a French Canadian working for the French radio station CFNS. 'We cannot always count on the same people to defend our rights and more than often our own compatriots turn their backs to us.' We are discussing the strike of a few French-Canadian families in Saskatoon two years ago. 'To pacify us, we were given a bilingual school. Twenty-seven French-Canadian children, under the direction of one teacher, are allowed to play and to sing in French one hour daily.'

'But how do you in Alberta and Saskatchewan speak such good French?'

'We nurse our French, madame, and we respect it. But unfortunately,' she says rather bitterly, 'when young Quebeckers arrive here to work with us, their language is inferior, sometimes vulgar.'

How guilty we are in Quebec of having neglected to purify our language, of having allowed so many *anglicismes* in our conversations. We in Quebec have much to be forgiven by our French-Canadian compatriots living away from what I like to think is their motherland.

The wind howls on the prairies; the whirling dust darkens our clothing and nearly chokes us. We are obliged to close all our windows to be able to breathe easily. We are both silent, oppressed by this heavy climate. The land is flat, and lies straight and naked to the horizon. If only I could plant men in Canada as one plants roses in a deserted garden!

Before this trip, I had anticipated that our concept of national unity would differ from that of the English provinces, but still I felt a certain admiration for what I had imagined to be a Canadian solidarity. I have greatly changed my opinion since, and I have lost confidence in English Canada's open-mindedness. It is easy for the other provinces to accuse Quebec of narrow nationalism, but because each province thinks it is better than the other, there are ten Canadas, each little concerned with unity but aggressively sure that it is the only one in the right.

It is quite difficult to differentiate between Calgary, Edmonton, and Saskatoon. Politically these three towns are not alike, but visually they are easily confused. Regina stands out because of the serenity of its Municipal Park, 'our pride and our glory'. Here, flowers and trees, lakes and lawns, ducks and water-hens converse together in superb indifference to human beings. In the centre of this oasis stands Parliament. André and I are both impressed by its conservative and Victorian splendour.

'To understand Saskatchewan', Woodrow Lloyd, leader of the Opposition, slowly and prudently observes, 'one must keep in mind the ethnic mosaic of this province.' André begins to smoke nervously and dares not look at me. I quietly close my notebook: once again I am going to hear the same story about egalitarian policy, the Canadian mosaic, *et cetera*. Mr. Lloyd does not compromise himself; I ask him if he shares Premier Thatcher's idea concerning a strong central government, but he evades my question with a smiling serenity. How I wish I could feel as sure as all these English-speaking Canadians, that they have inherited by fate or by God some kind of ancestral truth. 'In Regina, we recognize the equality of all Canadians'; but a few hours ago, I was told by New Canadians how hard it was for them to be accepted by the Anglo-Saxon *minority*. I seriously doubt this so-called partnership between all races.

'Moral barriers still exist in the rural districts and we must be prudent. In Quebec, you want to go too fast.'

He is right. In Quebec, we are in a hurry. We have no time to lose, we are busy building, repairing, studying. As quietly and prudently as my host, I interrupt our interview. Though I am more than grateful to be received with such cordiality everywhere I go, today I cannot endure much more expression of prudence, more cautious advice, more paternalism. Granted, in Quebec, we do a million things wrongly, but at least we do something! In some parts of Canada, I feel as if I were living in slow motion. Suddenly it seems urgent for André and me to hear new words, bold ideas about Canada and its future. And a little sense of humour would help.

'What does the youth of Saskatchewan think of Quebec?' I ask a young journalist.

'They could not care less,' she answers promptly.

The young people here are not concerned, it appears, with Canadian politics. They want a good job, a sense of security, and a life without complications. Maybe this is the ultimate goal of all English Canadians.

A few months ago, a well-known politician stated during a N.D.P. political meeting: 'If only it were possible to put a rope around Quebec and pull it to the middle of the ocean in order never to hear from it again.' I suppose if I had been a more alert journalist or a less discreet woman I could have somehow forced my interlocutors to admit the same thing. I would have to be deaf to words and to voices not to hear, underneath polite

81

discussions, the grumbling of prejudices, of animosity. And this same undercurrent of contempt grips many French Canadians in Quebec.

We have just had a wonderful dinner: this experience has been rare lately, and it is worth a few lines in this diary. In Canada we differ not only in language, but also in our eating habits. To each his own way to eat, surely. I do not wish to change the customs of the English provinces, but there exist for people sensitive to good food certain basic laws of gastronomy which should be observed. More and more Europeans will visit Canada. They are not more intelligent, more *raffiné* than we, but surely they are gourmets as we are not. Because this country has nothing much to offer them in terms of places to visit, we should do our best to provide them with excellent meals. Quebec's restaurants and bistros are not all a gourmet's paradise, but in general our hotel owners are doing their best to educate our people to eat better food and enjoy better wines. Incidentally, in English as in French Canada I have met wonderful 'cordon bleus' who cooked excellent dishes. I remember with pleasure a salmon slowly cooked on charcoal in Vancouver, an English trifle in Calgary, and a shrimp soup in Prince Rupert, and I long for the recipes. But in most English provinces, one is served indifferently, and even the most expensive foods lack any real flavour. Day after day, we face baked potatoes with sour cream, nearly frozen salads with Thousand Island dressing, rubber bread, and soaked toast.

I shall never forget the horrified face of my French publisher Pierre Tisseyre when he told me Canadian wines were pasteurized! If we do not take the trouble to prepare decent food and to provide good wines at a reasonable price, we will not enjoy the reputation of being hospitable.

Once again our car rolls past empty lands, deserted farms, stunted trees. 'We have four hundred miles to drive before Winnipeg,' sighs André. We are both tired, silent, anxious to get home. I write my diary on my briefcase resting on my knees.

The difficult equality between Canadians does not apply only to French and English Canadians; the 'third group' consisting of New Canadians also has a chip on its shoulder. Not easily accepted by those who believe in a Canadian mosaic, they fear the emergence of French Canadians and they tend to discriminate against this 'second group'. Because they are separated from their native land as well as from their culture, they try hard to retain their language and their customs in Canada. Before they were given their citizenship, they must have studied our history. How can they deny the fact that French-Canadian rights are fundamental in this country?

MANITOBA

Canada [in 1871]
was, however, a nation
projected rather than
a nation formed.

W. L. Morton,
The Canadian Identity

Everywhere in English Canada, French Canadians live and have survived; but nowhere, outside Quebec, have I found the presence of French Canada. How to construct its destiny?

By building its future on the creation of a strong National Federation of French-Canadian Minorities. By grouping the numerous pale and sentimental French weeklies called *L'Alouette, La Survivance, Le Patriote*, etc., into a bold, strong newspaper, titled something like *Présence Française*, with an eastern and a western edition.

I am finally convinced that Quebec cannot 'constitutionally' help our French minorities in any other way than financially. The more we consider the privileges of our own English minority in Quebec, the more we can predict the fight, and its chance of success, for the rights of the French minorities throughout Canada.

Midnight
WINNIPEG

We have spent our first evening in Winnipeg with some

old friends and they startled us with their views on Quebec and on Canada.

'What has Ottawa done to make us proud of being Canadians?'

'Why should nine provinces be made to change their attitudes and their way of life for the sake of one?'

'Quebec is pushing too hard and we won't cater to you.'

'Language is the only link we have with other Canadians.'

This peculiar conversation, I was told hours later, was intended to 'provoke my reactions'. I have none. Tonight, I am, as the boxers say, punch-drunk.

May 29
3 p.m.
WINNIPEG
University of Manitoba

Suddenly all my fears and my anxiety for the Canadian dilemma are expressed by Professor W. L. Morton, head of the department of history at the University of Manitoba. 'I am today more ready than I ever was to accept the cultural duality of Canada, but if we must be forced into political duality, then I think it would be best for Quebec to secede.' A very simple phrase, which points irrevocably to our different views on the constitution.

'You would rather break Canada than share its destiny with us,' I answer quite bitterly, and then I go on to say, 'If an historian of your reputation and of your authority thinks along these lines, I really do not see what I am doing in your country. I might as well go home, and say quite definitely in answer to the question of my book, that my country is Quebec.'

Professor Morton is quite disturbed by my emotional outburst. He tries hard to make me see his point and I also try to express my own views on a real partnership of French and English Canadian. I am a little intimidated by him. I have read most of his books and am fully aware that my historical knowledge is very limited compared to his.

'You will have to forgive my sweeping statements,' I apologize. 'My opinions on Quebec and on Canada stem more from intuition than from any research.'

Professor Morton assures me of his indulgence and for hours we debate the Canadian question with friendship and honesty but with opposed views. I point out to him how deeply involved our intellectuals are in Quebec's revolution. 'Yours', I go on to say, 'are suspicious of politics; they prefer to criticize than to join a party. In Quebec, our writers, novelists, poets, historians, sociologists are keeping pace with our social upheaval. Duplessis used to despise them, but today they form the avant-garde of our political thinkers.'

I recall for him the roles of Gérard Pelletier, Jean Marchand, and Jacques-Yvan Morin, of Michel Brunet and many others who left the security of their academic milieu to mix and work with our people. There is a great difference between the philosophy of our labour leaders and those of English Canada. Ours are concerned, of course, with bettering wages, but they are also implicated in Quebec's social life.

I am quite grateful to have met Professor Morton. I now know that the English will never consent to Quebec's becoming an associate state with Canada, but I am still very moved at having heard Professor Morton say as a last good-bye: 'I am going to Trent University to become president of the Champlain College and I have every intention of having the college live up to its name. It will become, I hope, a real bicultural home.'

10 p.m.
WINNIPEG

'Here, we must transform our ethnic group into a real French cultural milieu,' observes Paul-Emile Leblanc, a young, energetic Franco-Manitoban. 'We lose fifty per cent of our French youth every year; they all emigrate to Quebec. This brain-drain does not worry Manitoba; one more or one less French Canadian here does not make much difference,' he says with regret, 'but this province is losing its best minds.' And once again I listen in silence to his accounts of the difficulties of this French-Canadian group. 'Please inform the Cultural Affairs

88

Ministry how happy we would be if they were to pay the cost of an airmail edition of *Le Devoir*.' I shall, for I support their suggestion.

Dick Malone, vice-president and editor of the Winnipeg *Free Press*, comes for a drink with André and me. I am wary of this meeting because I have been told that he feels little sympathy for Quebec, or for Catholics.

I am particularly interested by his efforts to have his daughter learn French. Like many other English Canadians honestly eager to encourage their children to become bilingual, Dick Malone met with insuperable difficulties.

'I had to send my daughter to Switzerland,' he fumes. 'Where do you think I could have sent a Protestant English daughter in Quebec?'

Where indeed? But fortunately such bigotry is over. The priest-ridden province has rid itself of its over-religious prose-lytism.

He and my husband debate the merits of American investments, and I am keenly interested in their opinions. Their discussion turns to Walter Gordon's book, *A Choice for Canada*. Dick Malone refutes Gordon's theory. While listening to their divergent points of view, I begin to suspect that one of the schisms between French and English Canada rests on the fact that Quebec wants too much independence and the rest of the country too little. But I dare not express this discovery out loud.

'I am not worried about foreign capital, provided we learn to manage our own affairs,' says Dick Malone. And he adds, for André's happiness, 'We are afraid of our own power.'

Addressing himself to me, he goes on: 'When the Hudson's Bay Company bought Morgan's in Montreal, they were shocked to realize how few people in the management could speak French. Within a few weeks they were all sent to learn French.'

'Will you allow me to quote your dissaffection for the English minority in Quebec?'

'Yes. They have been very stupid in the past. They should have told us long before what went on in Quebec.' He adds, 'We welcome French Canadians in the West, but divorced from their Church.'

And suddenly I am angry. Am I less sensitive because for

over a hundred times I have listened to what French Canadians should do, not do, say or not say? 'We like you, but . . . .' 'We welcome you but . . . .'

'You want French Canadians on the condition that they do not disturb your splendid English way of life.'

'We resent being pushed.'

So do I. And we hotly debate the issue for two hours. We part friends, but I think I may have hurt his feelings.

Sunday
May 29
WINNIPEG

It would be inconceivable for a French Canadian travelling through Winnipeg and St. Boniface not to pay her respects to Madame Pauline Boutal who for forty-one years has directed the French drama group called Le Cercle Molière. Her troupe has been awarded many trophies from the Dominion Drama Festival and has won honour and admiration from all of French Canada.

'St. Boniface is becoming more and more English,' she says. She talks proudly of her actors, but regrets that so many are leaving Le Cercle Molière to try their luck in Montreal.

'We have more liberty now to choose our repertoire. We are even beginning to play Sartre,' she smiles.

We exchange views on the theatres of French and English Canada and Madame Boutal commends the recital of our talented Claude Léveillé, singer from Quebec.

'Our young people know his songs,' she says proudly. 'They gave him an ovation, but,' she adds sadly, 'during the intermissions they all spoke English together.'

Voilà. There, by the grace of English Canada, goes the maternal tongue of hundreds of us.

'It would be a crime to launch our Franco-Manitobans in life without preparing them to meet every challenge from our English compatriots,' a lawyer states quite seriously. 'Here bilingual schools answer our problems.'

His friends confess how tired they are with *la cause*, with being struggling French Canadians in Winnipeg. 'From now on, we will stress the French aspect of Canadian culture.'

Good luck, *camarades*!

I hear of an English backlash here, of a hardening against Quebec since Premier Lesage toured Canada. Maybe it would be simpler for most of us to stay at home.

André is back at the wheel and drives carefully on a deserted route. We are both once again silent, but our silence is one of tenderness. I need these long hours of peace and of solitude to sort out my emotions, beside my *compagnon* who has been attentive and patient for twenty-five years.

We are staying tonight in Marathon, a name indicative of my present occupation. I too am engaged in a marathon in search of my country's soul. I have not found it yet.

We left Winnipeg very early this morning. It is a cosmopolitan city divided by the gap between its French and English population, a city of padded voices with multilingual accents, a city of numerous newspapers, of disparate opinions.

I remember the question of a young musician: 'Why do we English Canadians nearly always kill our artists? In Quebec you respect them more. Here we are more or less on probation.'

'But your Manitoba Theatre Centre is flourishing'.

'Yes, but Hirsch is leaving us.'

Many times, young English Canadians have complained to me of the dryness of their milieu, of its deafness to their ideals. Canadian artists are conscious of the dangerous brain-drain of English Canada, but they cannot create in a hothouse. Like all artists, they need space, freedom, love, trust, and maybe a bit of revolutionary spirit! We French and English have refused two revolutions: we in Quebec the French revolution of 1789, and the Upper Canadians the American one. Therefore, we are neutral, indifferent to the spirit of democracy; we have accepted conformity as our way of life and we even boast about it! Our religions, Catholic and Protestant alike, have anaesthetized our moral vigour. We have adopted European traditions and refuse to create our own. Not only do we ignore the artistic, socio-logical, and democratic explosion of French and English masters whom we quote and copy most of the time, but we have closed our eyes on the splendour of our own emotions. We live here on borrowed time. In Quebec we respect and encourage our artists a little more because for the last ten years they have participated in our revolution.

NEWFOUNDLAND

*It is a riddle wrapped in a
mystery inside an enigma.*

Sir Winston Churchill

When I was twenty, my images of Canada were the red coats of the Royal Canadian Mounted Police, the fisherman's creel, the *tuque* and *ceinture fléchée* of Jean-Baptiste, and the mirroring of a red canoe on Lake Louise. I should have resigned myself to these simplified versions of Canada.

Today aside from the geographical and political dimensions of Canada, I can think only of planes, buses, long and deserted roads. In less than three hours I shall land in St. John's, Newfoundland, last port of call on my trans-Canadian trip. I know nothing of this island of mystery, fog, and poverty, and I have chosen not to divert my ignorance, thus hoping to discover without any prejudices the Newfoundlander's truth.

Once again, I am enriched by circumstances; my companion on this flight is a native Newfoundlander now residing in Montreal, and for two hours she is kind enough to explain her people and their philosophy.

6 p.m.
ST. JOHN'S

I can hardly believe that this town, this room, and this hotel are located in the heart of Newfoundland – Terra Nova. Of

94

500,000 islanders, 100,000 live in St. John's, a town similar to Halifax with its wooden houses washed out by salt, fog, and sea air. I admire Cabot Tower, where Marconi received his first telegraphic message in 1901.

Newfoundland reminds me of Quebec. Here too, churches, families, and a multiplicity of confessional schools are the bases of society. I am somewhat amazed to discover here a vast network of schools under the auspices of the Salvation Army. Like Quebeckers, Newfoundlanders have a sense of history and of the oppressor's injustices. First colony of the British Empire, Newfoundland was conquered by Sir Humphrey Gilbert in 1597 in the name of the great Elizabeth. For centuries the island remained a fisherman's heaven; it was inhabited by French, Portuguese, English, and Germans, and if we remember that Newfoundland's entry into Confederation dates from 1949, it is easy to imagine what kind of life these people lived. But Newfoundlanders are magnificently independent and proud. They voted 51 per cent for, 49 per cent against Confederation, and though their union with Canada helped them reduce their secular poverty, most of them regret, today, their lost freedom. On April 1, date of the alliance between Newfoundland and Canada, many flags fly at half mast, and many islanders wear dark ties.

'You come from Canada?' I am asked upon my arrival. 'My son goes to Canada to school,' continues someone else. An islander is a Newfoundlander first, then a Canadian. Where have I heard this point of view before?

Midnight
ST. JOHN'S

I have spent my first evening in St. John's with Dr. Alain Frecker, former Minister of Education. We converse in French. Born in St. Pierre et Miquelon of Newfoundland parents, Dr. Frecker has given to his wife a love of and a command of French.

'I do not believe that your government will ever touch the actual frontiers of Labrador. This would constitute a grave error and would create a dangerous precedent in Canada. The decisions of the Supreme Court are irreversible. When your geographers publish maps of Quebec without clearly indicating our frontiers, we are furious and we have every right to be.'

I learn with joy that French Canadians living in Labrador are studying French with a Quebec curriculum.

'We have not been able in the past to give the French Canadians living in Labrador a really good French education but we wanted to in case one day some of them wished to go back to Quebec. Through transactions between the iron-ore company, Paul Gérin-Lajoie, and my ministry, we were able to reach an agreement and everyone seems to be happy.'

This example could be profitable to the other provinces in which French Canadians make up a sizeable minority. It is easy to understand that each province, having its own system of education, could not afford to publish its own French textbooks for minorities. Here I can almost hear people saying, 'But Quebec's education is too religious, too backward for our citizens.' This objection was true, years ago; tomorrow our province will adopt one of the most progressive systems of education in the world.

Dr. Frecker tells me of his anxieties that a modern education is much too anti-religious. 'Between a system of education controlled by the Church and one deprived of spiritual values, there should be a place for a Christian outlook,' he says. For me, the Parent Report on Education is profiling precisely this idea for Quebec.

'Your system of education in Quebec is in many aspects superior to ours,' states Dr. Frecker. 'Your schools may not have turned out as many technicians, scientists, economists, and financiers as those of Ontario, for example, but your determination has turned you into a nation which English Canada must now recognize. We have not yet achieved this sense of nationhood. Here in Newfoundland we think we have it, but the rest of Canada is still searching for a definite identity.'

I must be dreaming! For the first time in months, I am not obliged to defend our education against prejudices, against the many faults we have ourselves denounced.

Since my arrival, I have heard this observation: 'Every province in Canada is different, but Newfoundland is more different.' And of course this is automatically followed by, 'We may be Newfoundlanders first, but we support the good of Canada.' Today I realize that Canada as a whole does not exist, but is regionalized into eleven different republics. I write eleven, because English Quebec is an entity of its own on this continent.

July 21
5 p.m.
ST. JOHN'S

'We are the half-way house between the old and the new,' affirms Charles Perlin, editorialist and historian. 'Not long ago, we were a free nation, poor but proud. Since our entry into Confederation, in spite of our financial gains, we have acquired a sense of inferiority. Like Quebec, we have a sense of history, and we know the hardship of conquest. Defeated by Great Britain in 1583, dispersed by Sir John Burry in 1670, we gained an independent government in 1869, when we first rejected the idea of Confederation. In 1935, we lost our sovereignty and were governed by a commission formed by three Englishmen and three Newfoundlanders, and in 1949, sad event for most of us, we finally joined Confederation.'

The bitter history of Newfoundland moves me. On the island, Quebec is a remote reality and this ignorance is easily understood in the light of the hardship of the islanders.

'You are responsible for your own economic backwardness,' pursues Charles Perlin. 'You have lived within yourselves, interested in your own plight, and you have never played a positive role in Confederation. Today you want all you can get from Ottawa but you do not recognize that your industries have progressed through the financial help of the other provinces.'

I listen to him in silence, having lost all desire to argue. As the great Montaigne wrote, 'I do not propose, I expose.'

He continues, 'Newfoundland is a strategic point in Canada's defence. If we were under the command of a foreign power, we

97

would constitute a real menace for Canada. In a few years, we too will have our revolution. With the developments of Hamilton Falls, of the Brinco and the iron-ore companies, we too will know economic resurgence.'

Confederation Building
Office of the Premier

Confederation Building is the most important construction on this island. The architecture is rather functional, but it fits well into the general climate of the island. In the main hall there is an intriguing fresco. It depicts the story of Newfoundlanders with a bizarre assortment of Indians, English soldiers in costumes, and modern military equipment and airplanes. Past, present, and future are knit together in a painting definitely more folkloric than artistic.

I am now in the office of the premier, and if I can't see him I can indeed hear him! A dynamic man, I was warned, and this morning I can well believe it. Such a voice carries importance, no doubt. Mr. Smallwood is as popular here as W. A. C. Bennett in his own flowering province. The two men have much in common: they both put the interest of their provinces above all considerations and they are both ruthless pragmatists. But when Quebec premiers act with the same dedication for our province, the whole of this country gets in an uproar. I wonder why?

I have been cautioned not to mention the question of Labrador's frontiers if I want to make a good impression on the premier. He is quite sensitive to this subject and was greatly disappointed by the stand his friend Jean Lesage took on the issue.

I am beginning to feel void of any kind of enthusiasm for this vast and frightening country and I have to fight my own bitterness when I hear the same clichés repeated incessantly and with authority by people in authority. And suddenly when the premier's secretary tells me that Mr. Smallwood cannot receive me after all, I decide to go back to Quebec the next day. I am no longer able to judge anything in the right perspective. I hate injustices, but I have lost faith in Canada's own sense of justice. I will end this enquiry.

A last meeting with a journalist makes me aware of the strange bond between people of the same trade. Cassie Brown asks numerous questions on Quebec, and though I felt I had nothing more to say, I relax with her and let my hair down. I am suddenly bursting with words, thoughts, and Cassie laughs because ten minutes before I had warned her that I felt empty of ideas, of emotions. We are supposed to stay together for less than an hour and our dialogue continues late into the night. Soon we leave Canada to the Canadians, and discuss, as two women, love, husbands, children. It proves that French or English, all women in the world are interested in the same emotions.

I shall see the premier after all. I am introduced to him at the airport, and discover that we shall travel together. Decidedly I live under a lucky star.

Mr. Smallwood's conversation, however, ends my numerous interviews with English Canadians on a sour note. If I could have anticipated his attitude toward Quebec, I would have been much wiser not to seek a meeting with him. Like many others, he refuses any kind of equality with Quebec.

'If the pretensions of Quebec to think itself equal with the rest of this country were not so ridiculous, I would die with laughter,' states the premier of Newfoundland. He goes on to say bluntly what I had implied sadly to a French-Canadian journalist attached to *La Presse* of Montreal on June 11, that individually a French Canadian is extremely well received everywhere in

Canada, but collectively we are not accepted.

'The French Canadian is one of the most lovable human beings in Canada, but collectively he deserves a swift kick.' With this elegant thought, the premier continues without realizing my anger.

'Your politicians always need to pull the tail of the lion; they love to underline our own stupidity, but they do not frighten me. I let them say all they want about the frontiers of Labrador, but when Jean Lesage declares that Quebec might not respect the Supreme Court's decision on our boundaries, he makes a fool of himself. His *politique de grandeur* goes to his head, and he loses touch with reality.'

I listen to him in a furious silence with a kind of an insulting politeness, but intent on his thoughts, the premier goes on: 'Your politicians pay lip-service to your intellectuals, to their voters. But they don't mean what they imply. The day your province decides to leave Canada, they will be committing suicide. I have met your new premier, and he [Daniel Johnson] appears to be a very practical and simple kind of man. I got along quite well with him. He will be restful at our provincial conferences. Beside him, the grandiloquent Lesage appears completely ridiculous.'

On these wise words, I go back to my seat, and to my native Quebec. I do not judge English-speaking Canada on Mr. Smallwood's immortal thoughts, but somehow he has said quite bluntly what many people have uttered with a great deal of subtlety but perhaps less honesty.

Farewell, Newfoundland.

100

QUEBEC

A dominated people kept apart from great problems and decisions has nothing more to express than its revolt and its solitude.

André D'Allemagne,
Le Colonialisme au Québec

I am at the very end of this long journey into the past, into history and geography, and I am back to my initial question: Is my country Quebec or Canada? If I take into consideration the numerous people entrenched in their prejudices, in their assumptions that Canada is one nation only, then I should answer, my country is Canada! Thus I would win the praise of millions of English-speaking Canadians blindly convinced that only their language, their culture, their national and international politics are worth while on this continent. For the Québécois comfortable in his hatred of *les Anglais*, and equally convinced of his own cultural superiority in Canada, my answer should of course be, my country is Quebec, *bien sûr*. It is not possible to settle this question once and for all because no one in Canada has any definite solutions. Neither French nor English Canadians know what kind of future they would like to live in.

So tonight I shall rely on my experiences during this long voyage, and shall try to find some equilibrium between the two founding nations of Canada.

I am definitely not in the possession of simple national, constitutional, political, or ethical truths. I have not found The Solution to our numerous problems. But through the conversations I have had with hundreds of Canadians throughout Canada, and because of the many places I have visited or revisited, I have slowly become aware that if Canada is beautiful and exciting in a geographical sense, it is not on a human level.

Canada is inhabited by people of American, European, or other origins, and these Canadians are in turn Protestants, Catholics, Methodists, Anglicans, French, English, liberals, conservatives, socialists, nationalists. But where is their humanity behind these qualifications? We Canadians of different ethnic backgrounds have lost our simple respect for Man, for his identity, his richness and his poverty. But to respect a man is to know him.

Such knowledge, however, does not necessarily stem from trips taken by Canadians across the country. Yes, travel informs youth, but the journeys of Canadians who have firmly decided to pack in their suitcases their special brand of prejudices will not serve national unity. They will only encourage new and very temporary friendships. I have made some wonderful friends in Vancouver, Calgary, Edmonton, Winnipeg, Halifax, but because of them, am I more inclined to accept Ottawa's views on Confederation? Canadians will never really mix because each of us, French and English, arrive at a rendezvous absolutely convinced that we are in the right. Two hours of conversation with a man concerned about Quebec will not obliterate two centuries of prejudice. It would be infinitely more profitable to track down prejudices on all sides before trying to assess the man underneath his own special coat of history. In Canada, prejudices stem from all parts of the country and house themselves as much in the French as in the English expression of our Canadianism. Beyond our political and cultural differences, we are prisoners of history. Centuries of wars, defeats, and victories have divided France and England.

Many of us Canadians are the descendants of these two great nations more often at war than at peace with each other. Between the battle of Hastings and the famous battle on the Plains of Abraham there is no common measure, but between conquered and conqueror, hatred and the desire for revenge are always stronger than the concessions made through a peace

103

treaty. Between French and English Canadians, divergences are hereditary, historical, political, and irreducible. We must recognize our ancestral differences and cease to wish for some understanding between us, based not on a melting-pot theory but on some illusion of sharing a loving-cup which would turn dear enemies into dear friends.

And to put an end to these insupportable conversations on 'who won on the Plains of Abraham', I shall quote a letter written to me by a French-Canadian friend: 'With regard to this famous battle still going on between French and English in Canada, you should answer this: Do you mean to say that to erase the scars of battle between the mercenaries of the King of France and the King of England, not between French and English Canadians because at this time there was one Canada and it was French, you wish to settle our present problems with another war?'

In turn, the French Canadians who constantly refer to the Conquest to explain their traumas and their secular difficulties are, in my belief, as unrealistic as those English Canadians who incessantly ask who won over whom anyway?

In 1966, one can safely answer, only the Americans won.

France and England have definitely been more generous toward one another than most of our English-French lords who have invested themselves with the authority of breaking this country. After the Conquest, various Establishments controlled Canada and they still do today. These Establishments are French and English, Catholic and Protestant. They share a common desire to control and use the poor to enlarge their fortunes. My explanations are too simple, too biassed, too pat, but I am desperately fed up with the numerous books by experts who set out to explain not Canada's duality but Canada's rivalry. Disguised behind noble phrases and constitutional amendments, an English thought still lingers on: 'I hold the pot of gold and I shall not let go.' Therefore I feel free to observe that democracy, more than our Constitution, is sick in Canada.

. . . we suggest that all Canadians examine closely the concept of democracy itself. Too often, it has been reduced to the simple game of majority versus minority. Some English-speaking citizens before the Commission invoked the 'law of the majority' as though they were brandishing a threatening weapon; some French-speaking people, who had complained bitterly of the consequences of this 'law', expressed the desire to make use of it to their own advantage in a more or less independent Quebec.

This quotation, from the Preliminary Report of the Bi-Bi Commission, hems in the realities of our problems. Since many English Canadians have accused the commissioners of trying to break up this country, we can therefore assume that English Canada will never re-evaluate its own definition of democracy in order to ignore its own failure in understanding Quebec's views on Confederation. No commissioner, no expert will ever succeed in convincing the majority of Canadians of their sickness because most of them refuse to admit its symptoms. I have not yet perceived a real anxiety in English Canada. Our compatriots look with irritation on the frictions between Quebec and Ottawa because the tensions between one province and the central government emulate other tensions in other provinces. English Canada on the whole, except for a few intellectuals and journalists, is convinced of never having sinned against a democratic Canada which should be bicultural, bilingual, and, I hope one day, bi-national.

The defeat of democracy does not rest only on the shoulders of English Canada. Pushed to extremes by Anglo-Saxon arrogance, French Canada, in turn, wants to impose its own vision of democracy on Canada's fiscal, cultural, constitutional, and national policies. And it would certainly not be indiscreet to write that French Canadians are not all born with an instinctive respect for their neighbour's liberties. I well remember the general outcry in Quebec when French Canadians readily confessed their wish to send their children to non-confessional schools. All the Savonarolas of our society rose up to defend the religious liberty in our province. Our political leaders angrily sued and pursued the Jehovah's Witnesses less than ten years ago. The warm and respectful welcome their hundreds of delegates received in Montreal a few months ago proves our courage in re-assessing our ideas of religious democracy.

We still have to amend our political democracy. Once again, I shall leave to the experts, commissioners, and political journalists the privilege of putting into clear words the evidence of our sins against democracy. I shall point out only the rejection by some French Canadians of all compromise with Ottawa, and the choice of many English Canadians to remain blind to their own faults. As proof of our lack of respect for the individual's freedom, I shall refer to the ugly correspondence that accumulates on my working table each time I come back home after having spent some time in other provinces. From Western Canada, I have received numerous letters advising me 'to stay in Quebec from now on, to lead [my] province out of Confederation once and for all, because [we] in Quebec never added much to Canada since [we] are all a bunch of terrorists'.

From Quebec, many letters accuse me of being a turncoat, a dangerous 'bourgeoise and capitalist', of selling out to English Canada, and I am warned that a firing-squad is waiting for me on the morning of our first 'Independence Day'. These accusations are not very serious, but they point to our lack of respect for the other person's point of view. For example, when Jean Lesage mentions the young separatists, he fumes with rage. Why? When on the other hand some separatists speak of the federalists, they often laugh at them. They become vulgar, violently impolite, and their tantrums always fail to convince our population of their sincerity. When English Canadians, in turn, do their utmost to ignore the identity of the French Canadians living in their provinces, are they respectful of the rights of a minority group? As human beings, French Canadians are neither better nor worse than their English counterparts. The new Quebec takes self-criticism in its stride. I wonder if English Canada is ready for self-examination?

August 2
MONTREAL

Many Québécois are impatient, disappointed because our revolution is suddenly too quiet, too weak to match their fervour

106

in living and their ambitions for the future. The different shades
of opinions, the hesitation to pass a final judgment on a society,
the loyalty of friendship appear to be out of tune with a world
in desperate need to find immediate solutions for all problems.
In spite of my strong attachment to Quebec and my certitude
that my native Quebec holds, receives, and will keep me forever,
I still feel a disturbing need to remain objective, serene, honest.
But how can I not judge severely the rich, haughty, and domi-
neering Anglo-Quebec society which, while loudly stating its
roots in Quebec, has ignored for more than a century the out-
standing features of French Quebec? I am not over-concerned
with its control of most of our industries. French Canadians
never had the tools to build a strong economy. English Quebeckers took over because there was nobody else to assume authority,
and if we had created schools for the study of economics and
finance sooner, we would have been able to take our place
sooner in the industrial world of Quebec. Sociologists have
explained the reasons for our financial chaos; but more modestly
and with more vehemence, I will say that my contempt for some
factions of Anglo-Quebec society does not stem from its control
over our business, but from its negative attitudes toward the
fundamental realities of our French province. For example, how
many English Quebeckers read *Le Devoir, Cité libre, Parti pris,
Socialisme 66*; look at channel 2, the CBC's French TV
station in Montreal; are members of Le Cercle du Livre de
France and clients of French-Canadian bookstores; know of the
roles of Canon Groulx and Fathers Dionne, O'Neil, and Léves-
que in our quiet revolution? How many were ever patients in
French hospitals, have shopped in Place St-Hubert or at Dupuis
Frères? How many read one French-Canadian novel a year?
To pretend to help Quebec by controlling industries in turn
controlled by Americans, while employing thousands of French
Canadians, does not suddenly transform a financial tycoon into
a benefactor of the nation.

On the other hand, it is utterly grotesque for a French Canadian to blame Westmount for all our troubles. I have lived in
this section of Montreal for years and between the bourgeois of
Ste-Catherine Road in Outremont and the rich man living on

The Boulevard, there is not much difference. The two types of capitalist have done their utmost to amass a fortune with the help of their workers. Before the trade unions stopped them from paying the lowest wages possible, they had no instinctive wish to respect the individual rights of their employees.

Members of the social set who take costly vacations in Florida, in California, or the Costa Brava, are all the same. French or English, they have placed their immediate needs before the needs of the nation. So if we must judge sometimes harshly the lives of the Westmounters, let us be decent enough to look on the other side of the Mountain and honestly say that the capitalist French Canadian is not much better. As a matter of fact he is often harder with his workers than most English Canadians ever dare to be.

I was born in such a bourgeois milieu; I am perfectly at ease in admiring its courage, its determination to maintain French-Canadian industries with French-Canadian money. I am aware of the dangers of competition with American and English-Canadian products, but I have often been scandalized by the silence of our businessmen, French and English, on the important question of education, culture, and national politics. Mesmerized by the pressures of the market, the businessmen fear that they may compromise their profits if they dare one single bold idea in their community. In Quebec, journalists, labourers, artists, writers, intellectuals, have declared war on our complacency; the country club crowd has never hidden its distrust of these 'egg-heads' who dare to push Quebec society into further social reforms.

A rumour persists in Quebec that many English Quebeckers are quietly leaving the province to transplant their industries to other provinces. If the rumour is true, of course we will suffer from this transfer of capital to other provinces. Education, social reforms, economic planning are costly and Quebec needs the investments of all its citizens. But if our English-speaking compatriots cannot accept the second place in Quebec's life, then they will be happier elsewhere. But they will be losers in a national sense and the whole country will tell them.

For more than two hundred years they have lived among us.

108

As a minority they have rarely paid us the honour of speaking our language, of sharing, even occasionally, our way of life because they did not need French to earn their living. The way they have dealt with their French-Canadian neighbours has not endeared them to our hearts, nor encouraged us to treat them with more courtesy, more friendship. They still have to prove to us that they are real Quebeckers; some of them are doing just that, and I must commend these few for their courage and their honesty.

It would be useless and childish to blame Anglo-Quebeckers for most of the stagnation of Quebec. For example, no English Canadians can be held entirely responsible for the poor quality of our everyday French. The wealthy French families of Quebec have been involved in the corruption of our French. The sons and the grandsons of *la bourgeoisie canadienne-française* deliberately spoke bad French, used a vulgar pronunciation, because they feared ridicule if they spoke a cultivated French. Such snobbishness no longer exists today, but ten years ago such was the case. Any reader of this diary can go every day at closing time to our richer convents and colleges, and he will be rather shocked by the loud and vulgar vocabulary of our young hopes for Quebec.

Though the young separatists may not be quite clear on how they will achieve independence, they speak quite clearly, and I am grateful for the purity of their French.

In his turn, the young English Canadian would be wiser not to criticize the language of his French-Canadian friends. My English is good enough to have noticed the faults of his own language tainted with brooklynisms, slang, and such. He is wrong if he thinks that a French Canadian who is well read and well travelled will be unaware of his faulty grammar.

So we arrive at a strange paradox: if French Canadians had taken better care of their mother tongue, they would not find themselves today in the humiliating situation of demanding respect from nine provinces for a language that they themselves have not always respected in the past. And to end my commentaries on bilingualism, which will never be possible in this country because this country does not want to live by it, I shall only say that I am now sure that a majority will never learn the language of a minority for the sake of saving a constitution. And the young separatist or the zealous nationalist who refuses to speak English, in spite of the fact that one day he might well be swallowed by more than twenty million Anglo-Americans, is the living example of absurdity. I speak English not to please English Canada, but because living on an Anglo-American continent offers me the resources of a second culture, and I simply refuse to be confined to one only. My bilingualism does not make me inferior or superior; it simply permits me to live in tune with the world around me.

August 6
MONTREAL

I have been living in a French house in Montreal for a few days, and I have suddenly stumbled against the tragic dichotomy of this great city. Montreal – a French town? No. A beautiful metropolis alive with gardens, trees, mountain, bistros, theatres, rich quarters, and historic streets, but alas also made ugly by the bad taste exhibited in its commercial advertising. I still wonder by what kind of illusion we speak of Montreal as being a model of the so-called Canadian mosaic! This big and flourishing city gives to Canada the vivid image of our segregated societies. Montreal is not united by cultures or shared activities. Each ethnic group goes its separate way. And it is difficult to understand why its French population licks the boots of its English minority and willingly uses English for most of its public signs. If Montreal is really the second biggest French city in the world, then I as a French Canadian must be made aware of it. I personally shudder when I think that soon millions of European tourists will laughingly take pictures of stores called 'Immaculée Conception Queen of Hot Dogs' rather than photographing the Expo sites, which will probably be too international to reflect the authenticity of Quebec. And I sometimes wish that our young Quebeckers who never miss an occasion to demonstrate against this or that, would organize sit-ins in front of those ugly signs rather than in insignificant restaurants whose menus

110

are in English only. Mayor Drapeau, who is one of the most dynamic personalities of Montreal, has perhaps chosen to remain blind to this shocking state of bilingualism.

For many French Canadians, the decisive hour for our future in or out of Confederation is about to toll. Like many of them, I am afraid, not of expressing my views on this matter, but of choosing unwisely. Because of this long and difficult journey into Canada, I know today quite definitely that at this precise moment of our national life, my country is not, and will not be, English Canada as I have seen it and heard it speak during the numerous meetings, lectures, and television and radio shows I have participated in for the last six months throughout nine provinces. I do not seem to fit anywhere into this haughty society, convinced of its superiority to my native Quebec. A few years ago, a radio broadcaster repeated incessantly that civic responsibility expressed itself through a host of little things. My farewell to English Canada also rests on a host of little unimportant things of no political or constitutional value, but so painful that their repetition has finally convinced me that though French and English Canada can still live under the same roof, they will never share the same bed. For a long time we have invented all kinds of excuses to explain this strange divorce. We live under the same constitution, we are governed by a central government, but we have never succeeded in fostering a sense of love between our two founding nations. Today, we French Canadians fully realize and denounce the fact that if English Canadians in general have refused to speak and to share with us, it is not as we have pretended for years because they are timid or introverted, or because they have a congenital difficulty in learning a second language. It is simply because, as every French Canadian who is sensitive fully knows, the English Canadian thinks himself instinctively superior to people of

111

French descent. Even the more open-minded English Canadian cannot accept the idea of two nations in Canada, and he will never tolerate political duality. He cannot conceive that fourteen million people can be equal to four million, and because he is three times stronger he naturally thinks himself three times superior. Even if by some unexpected miracle the B.N.A. Act could be amended so that French Canadians living outside Quebec would become equal to English Canadians, most historians, politicians, experts, intellectuals would never share with Quebec in the great decisions of Canada.

I will certainly not go over the events of our so-called quiet revolution, which was in fact so quiet that promises of witchhunting were enough to scare it away. Many books, articles, and essays have been published to extol the glory of the Lesage government, but we now know that this glory was not very solid, understood only by the intelligentsia of Quebec, and frowned upon by the less educated people of our province. The wind does not seem to favour us anymore: strikes paralyse our progress, and the proposed Sidbec steel plant, vital to our economic growth, was a political balloon that exploded because of hard statistics and hard realities. The young partisans of the R.I.N. who voted *Indépendantiste* are happy to have succeeded in dividing the votes, and they are unafraid of having thrown Quebec right back into the hands of the Union Nationale. And those who voted for Mr. Johnson because they wanted to achieve independence quickly will be very disappointed, I fear.

Of course Mr. Johnson commands our respect; but he will be kept busy by his numerous army of partisans who wait to be paid for their services and who will not hesitate to plunge Quebec into the Middle Ages in order to appease their fear of novelty. 'We are told of new politicians,' observed Gérard Pelletier in *Le Devoir* of August 6. 'I would like to believe they are numerous. But whom do we see at the commanding posts of our state? Neither Messrs. Bellemare, Lafontaine, Jean-Noël Tremblay, Vincent, or Dozois, nor Mr. Johnson himself can be presented as new faces. Today we see only Mr. Massé. It is not much.' And not reassuring either. After this fatal June 5, Mr. Lesage said that never in Quebec history had a government

112

faced such a strong and alert Opposition. Let us hope that these bright and bold men will acquire the patience to sit calmly on the Opposition bench, instead of finding new ventures to canalize their initiative. In a province where able men are scare, it would be a miracle if these leaders did not seek to use their abilities outside the political field. I hope they will not leave Quebec for Ottawa – because on the federal scene they will probably be offered secondary posts and in a few months some mysterious rumours will attempt to destroy their reputations.

The present Quebec needs all its men of goodwill. The Union Nationale government must be watched. Our premier does not say exactly what he wants to say; he flirts first with Equality, then with Independence, as he once wrote in a book. Therefore I think that the official and non-official opposition of the Union Nationale must be very alert. If to maintain his stand on Confederation Mr. Johnson talks of independence as a last resort for Quebec, then we will march to a premature independence achieved not through the collective will of the French-Canadian people, but through the political bluff of dangerous politicians.

I am quite aware that a few *Indépendant* sociologists have declared the secession of Quebec to be economically feasible. But there are simple, honest, naïve, human, non-political questions still unanswered to this day. For example, if Quebec were independent today, on whose gold or silver could we base our money? We are presently near bankruptcy; it would indeed be surprising to find tomorrow, in view of the bitterness that our decision to leave Confederation would spread, the money needed to stabilize our economy. Where would we find the funds to support our national debt, to build our defences, to raise an army to protect our frontiers? How and with what collateral would we negotiate an agreement with the Americans over the Seaway they helped to finance? And if Eaton's of Montreal wanted to import from Eaton's of Toronto, would the Quebec store pay duty? And if Ontario wished to trade with the Maritimes or the Maritimes wished to export to Western Canada, would these provinces or states be made to pay some taxes to pass over and through Quebec? How would Quebec's government be able to pay for its labour without once again obliging

113

the workers to carry the cost of our delusions of grandeur? Surely the industries, whether English or American, would not leave Quebec if their business were good, but tomorrow would we be able to recruit in Quebec the manpower needed to run them? And because such a small country, powerfully surrounded by Canada and the U.S.A., could not afford to pay the same high wages as the Americans and the Canadians, who would come to help us, to share in our debts, to orient our disorientation? If today Quebec does not offer much to immigrants from France, are we dreamers enough to think that in five or ten years they will leave behind a Europe divided by wars and revolutions to come to a poor country divided by wars and revolutions? Do we have the right to hope for such conditions, to lead our people into such chaos, such misery?

But if in spite of these hard facts, we French from Quebec and from the diaspora still wish to realize this independence, then for years we will have to go back to school, to anchor our dreams in cold reality, to discipline our emotions and re-evaluate our notions of democracy, of culture, of humanism, of the right of men and nations to self-determination. If tomorrow once again the labourers, the workers, the small people, pay for our desire to be free and independent, history will condemn the separatists of today because they were probably too young, too emotional, to realize that the fate of a nation does not rest only on its artists, its *chansonniers*, its intellectuals, its students, but mostly on the security and the social welfare of its working class. Jean Paul Sartre wrote: 'Man is to be created, and man alone can create man.' In this perspective, French Canada is to be created, and only French Canadians can create it. For the last three or four years we have talked enough about *Indépendance*; we must begin to work for it, not only politically but also humanly and with all the moral strength we possess, if we want to keep this utopian independence. We must also convince our friends and our brothers of the importance of this option, not with gestures of violence or death, but by proving the ability of our hands to carve the political and economic cornerstones of our future.

Tonight, sadly, I do not believe any more that English Canada will share with us the Canadian destiny, and I do not believe that French Canadians are sufficiently aware of the dark hours ahead for them if they want to achieve the independence of the nation. The actual leaders of too many separatist movements are responsible by their selfishness and their empty speeches for the tragic ignorance of most Quebeckers *vis-à-vis* the numerous sacrifices we will have to consent to in order not simply to obtain independence but to maintain it.

But from now until the day Quebec may secede, what will French and English Canadians do? They will certainly continue to criticize each other happily, but in constitutional terms, *bien sûr*! They will also continue to affirm quietly that this country is in good health, that its frontiers are open to all men regardless of race or creed. And around the peace tables of this world, politicians and statesmen will wear their hypocritical masks and pretend with smiling and benevolent faces that they are qualified mediators between the poor underdeveloped nations and the rich who have not yet learned to share their bread with their black or white brothers.

September 12
LAC MAROIS
La Cédraie

I shall end this diary by noting the similarities between French and English societies both subjected to cultural, economic, and political pressures. *Vis-à-vis* the U.S.A., English Canada does not exist politically; economically it offers to the Americans some good possibilities for investment which allow them to reaffirm their strength on this continent.

Vis-à-vis English Canada, French Canada has no political power either, but the economic development of our province rests on English and American capital. Thus, French and English Canadians are satellites of the Americans and we are both in danger of becoming more and more Americanized. The only difference between our two nations is that we in Quebec hold desperately to our identity, while English Canada does not yet fully understand the meaning of one. But our two national weaknesses do not make a political force. If years ago we had only

115

studied our qualities instead of harping on our respective faults, Canada would probably not be a more united nation; but at least it would have more strength to fight American pressures and to convince Canadians not to seek radical answers to difficult and long-standing problems.

Here I must confess that I am not very good at adopting a constitutional or juridical language to speak about our Canadian crisis. But I must say that even if the true spirit of the B.N.A. Act signed in 1867 did not allow for the presence of two political nations in Canada, it is no longer possible in 1967 to ignore the two branches of the Canadian tree. Quebec is not and never will be a province *comme les autres*, because four million human beings live, think, speak, and fight in a political and cultural climate completely different from that of the nine other provinces. Even when Donald Creighton, the high priest of constitutional matters, writes in arrogant anger, 'French-Canadian nationalism could be carried to the point at which English Canada would finally decide in disgust and indignation that it had had enough,' English Canada will still have to face the fact that we have survived, we are the second-largest majority in Canada, and we have the right to speak in our own country.

Since Quebec forms a society in constant evolution, her needs in 1967 cannot be fulfilled by a constitution ratified one hundred years ago. As long as Quebec will be compelled to act as a province, there will be tensions between our provincial government and the federal one, and within a few months we will come to a constitutional impasse endangering the life of the whole nation. Yes, independence for Quebec would be the ideal solution for those of us tired of not being able to feel at home in our own country. But English Canada is not ready to fight alone against the American giant; and Quebec is no more ready to assume alone the destiny of four million people, because these four million French Canadians have chosen to dream their fate rather than work to better it in their everyday lives.

This is why, if English Canada can never be my country because it refuses to accept my language and culture and refuses to share with me Canada's future, Quebec therefore is *ma patrie*. But Quebec is not yet a country. My own com-

116

patriots have not so far created structures for our political, cultural, and economic independence. If I analyse the failures of our societies, I cannot resist pointing out that we form two worlds in agony. An independent Quebec that in twenty years could no longer assume its liberty would die in the arms of irate Americans furious at being obliged to add our problems to theirs. And an English Canada economically weak could not survive if it were cut in two by Quebec's secession. In consequence, French and English Canadians who, for the sake of superiority, revenge, or racial prejudices refuse to accept the reality of our collective weaknesses will, tomorrow, be held responsible for Canada's death.

Yes, I am pessimistic, but I defy my reader to live for months among people who have nothing much in common and to come out of this experience without being morally bruised. Like all French-Canadian nationalists, I would love to write firmly that my country is Quebec, but again I face the problem that Quebec as a country does not exist. And I will not create it with words of anger, with dreams, with love or hatred; I will not invent a country by refusing to live in step with an Anglo-American rhythm, by justifying my hunger for freedom, or by seeking revenge because Ottawa has refused to give what I considered vital. Quebec will become a country only when the whole nation wants it.

To determine with lucidity what Quebec really wants, the Estates General of French Canada has been founded. Jacques-Yvan Morin, a lawyer and professor of international law attached to the University of Montreal, has defined it as 'a meeting of the representative elements of the nation'. The Estates General of French Canada wants to become the focus of a vast forum of French-Canadian opinions, the meeting-point of all the strength of a nation who want to study its situation and to define its vital orientation. In the spring of 1967, through these Estates General, French Canada will choose among a 'particular status', 'co-operative federalism', associate statehood, and independence.

These four options make me wonder: if I forget the already dead 'co-operative federalism', I begin to suspect that the best solution for problems confronting us for years to come might

117

be to adopt a special status that will eventually lead us to the concept of associate states modelled on the Federation of Switzerland. I already hear the loud protest of my English-speaking friends who will accuse me of wanting too much too quickly. But I feel that the time is ripe to ask for too much and very quickly. If English Canada does not give Quebec a more important place in the constitution, then yes, we will run to an independence for which neither French nor English Canada is prepared. I have no intentions of blackmailing anyone with these remarks; I have studied some facts and I simply give them their logical evaluation.

When I began this diary I stated: 'What I will write about Canada will not change Canada.' How little did I know on that night of February 1966 how much my trip would transform me. More than my publishers and my readers, I am fully conscious that the task of inventing solutions to unify a country divided into ten republics is too much for a single human being. I am also aware that though I have tried to remain serene and objective, I have probably not reported all I have heard and seen, nor have I been able to study extensively the imperatives for each province. But for more than six months, I have looked in all sincerity for a common denominator between French and English Canadians, and I have not found one.

Consequently, I have come back to my land, *ma Terre-Québec*, more *Québécoise* than *Canadienne*, because I have learned harshly, with pain and anguish, that to remain true to my past, to my culture, to my language, and to the very French individual that I have become, I must live in Quebec, in a Quebec that one day may yet become my *country*.

SOLANGE CHAPUT ROLLAND

Foreword to the French edition

by CLAUDE RYAN

This book describes, more clearly than a great many abstract theses, a most important aspect of the present-day reality both of Quebec and of Canada.

The trip that Solange Chaput Rolland has just taken through English Canada really serves as no more than an intelligent and appropriate pretext. Behind the story of her travel we must read the account of an entire life that has now reached its maturity.

Solange Chaput Rolland embarked upon life much as she embarked upon her trip through Canada. From textbooks of history she gleaned the main facts about Canada. Despite certain episodes that were less than edifying, she retained, on the whole, an impression that was optimistic. A French Canadian attached above all to her province of Quebec, she nevertheless believed in the validity of the Canadian experience. Of middle-class background, she soon had the opportunity of establishing contact with English Canada. All her life she was to be exposed, to a greater extent than most of her French compatriots, to the fire of frequent confrontation with the 'other' Canada.

119

For several years, Mme Chaput Rolland has felt a growing nationalistic fervour. 'I became a devoted nationalist,' she has written, 'following my experience as a journalist and as a lecturer in English Canada.'

In her case, therefore, there is no question of the kind of hot-house nationalism that is fostered in the security of a cultural ghetto. Usually, travelling appeases the fever that is the result of an enclosed environment. The French Canadian who leaves this environment generally comes back with more subtle, more moderate views.

In this case, the facts are entirely different. It was not Solange Chaput Rolland's first trip into English Canada. But she nevertheless wanted to set out with an entirely fresh mind in order to discover the English Canada of today. Without ever forgetting who she was herself and what she had become, she honestly wished to discover what other people were like, what they thought, and how they lived.

Her verdict is not very encouraging. Almost everywhere she discovered interesting signs of overture, especially in some intellectual or political circles. But on the whole her diagnosis remains pessimistic. The English Canada that she has just seen again is still dangerously turned inward, and more or less indifferent to the immense challenge of the rebirth of modern Quebec. When pushed, it is willing to admit that there is a problem somewhere. But it is incapable of pinpointing the real aspects of the problem, and still less of proposing valid solutions.

Solange Chaput Rolland, who is a sensitive person rather than a woman of action, concludes from her experience that it is impossible for the moment to find any common denominator between French and English Canada. 'I have come back to my land, *ma Terre-Québec*,' she writes, 'more *Québécoise* than *Canadienne,* because I have learned harshly, with pain and anguish, that to remain true to my past, to my culture, to my language, and to the very French individual that I have become, I must live in Quebec, in a Quebec that one day may yet become my *country*.'

I also have travelled a great deal throughout English Canada, and I cannot share the author's pessimistic conclusion. I attach

120

less importance or less significance to specific incidents that may have irritated me. For me, politics is based on reason more than on cultural affinities, and something tells me that the political societies of the future will be increasingly larger and more diversified than the cultures underlying them. Like Mme Chaput Rolland, I am conscious of the fierce resistance that prevents English Canada from understanding the terrible urgency of the Canadian crisis, but I am none the less aware of a very real progress that is being achieved in certain spheres and that may portend a more interesting future.

I must confess that I consider the whole of Canada as my country. I refuse to shut myself up in a cultural and political world that is artificially homogeneous, and from which I would in any case have to break out in order to establish (and in their language for the most part) economic and cultural links with my two hundred million neighbours. The inequality that irritates so many of my people seems to me, on the contrary, a tragic appeal to transcend the difficulties, an unavoidable invitation to accept the challenge of excellence as the only means of achieving our true fulfilment.

But I also know, and I can understand it, that a great ferment of affirmation is now at work in the consciousness of French Canada. It is a movement that had hitherto taken the form of a powerless protest, of a painful appeal to the other party's conscience and sense of justice. From now on, the movement centres upon one positive, very concrete aim: the total and exclusive possession of Quebec. French-Canadian inspiration had always lacked a dynamic vision of history, tending to the future. Such a pole now exists, and it is clearly perceived: the making of a society of French form in Quebec.

English Canadians may be tempted to say, reading Mme Chaput Rolland: 'She is dreaming. Her plan will founder upon the hard laws of economic reality.' When British journalists were making the same objection to me the other day, I suggested that they take a look at a map of Europe, and then tell me whether they had ever seen a grouping of countries or frontiers so little in accordance with economy or rational logic.

Political history is definitely dictated to a greater extent by human consent than by the geographical position of rivers or mountains. The blind exasperation of minorities sometimes leads them to gestures that are not very logical: instead of pure and rational theory, they often prefer, in the end, the apparent anarchy of free choice. The blind obstinacy of majorities, on the other hand, often results in the destruction of grandiose projects which would have been valid in themselves but for which, unfortunately, there was not the generosity of spirit and the profound acceptance of diversity that would have made sense of them.

I do not know how our own story will end. It may be that we shall stay together. It may be that we shall separate for a time, with the possibility of reuniting later on. I do not know what will happen. It is my belief, nevertheless, that a separation at this time would satisfy the ambitions of people of the author's background rather than the real interests, the terribly mundane, day-to-day interests of the ordinary man. I am afraid that if we exposed ourselves to a lowering of our standard of living, we would as a consequence expose ourselves to a significant limitation of our fundamental freedoms.

In this world of great economic, political, and technological assemblies in which we are called to live, nations must survive, for they continue to be valid expressions of the values that are dearest to man. I do not believe, however, that they are by themselves sufficient to determine the political boundaries of the future.

Mme Chaput Rolland's book has the great merit of challenging us to a painful examination of our conscience at the very moment when we are, whether we like it or not, about to make serious political decisions. It is a book that is the sincere cry of a troubled mind rather than a concrete and positive plan. Nevertheless, it expresses with eloquence, faithfulness, and realism a crucial dimension of the Canada of today. I hope that English Canadians will read it with loyalty and humility, and that French Canadians will study it realistically, and not come to premature conclusions in those places where the author, even though herself on the brink of an irreversible choice, has left the door slightly open for the future.